FRAMEWORK

Christianity and Life

RANGE HIGH SCHOOL
FORMBY

M.A. Chignell

Edward Arnold

© M.A. Chignell 1987

First published in Great Britain 1987 by
Edward Arnold (Publishers) Ltd
41 Bedford Square, London WC1B 3DQ

Edward Arnold (Australia) Pty Ltd
80 Waverley Road, Caulfield East
Victoria 3145, Australia

Reprinted 1987 (twice)

British Cataloguing in Publication Data
Chignell, M.A.
　Framework: Christianity and life.
　1. Christian life
　I. Title
　248.4　　BV4501.2

ISBN 0-7131-7526-5

All rights reserved. No part of this publication may be reproduced, stored in a retrieval system, or transmitted in any form or by any means, electronic, photocopying, recording, or otherwise, without the prior permission of Edward Arnold (Publishers) Ltd.

My love and gratitude as always to Barbara Windle without whose help this book would never have been written.

'Make everything as simple as possible, but not simpler.' (Einstein)

Text set in Century Schoolbook by BookEns, Saffron Walden, Essex

Printed by Butler and Tanner Ltd, Frome, Somerset
Bound by W.H. Ware and Sons Ltd, Clevedon, Avon

Acknowledgements

The Publishers would like to thank the following for their permission to include copyright material: the United Nations for an extract from *The Universal Declaration of Human Rights of the United Nations* (General Assembly resolution 217 A (III) of 10 December 1948); The General Synod of the Church of England for extracts from the Marriage Service in *The Alternative Service Book 1980* © Central Board of Finance of the Church of England which are reproduced by permission; William Heinemann Ltd for drawings from C. Padfield & F.E. Smith: *Law made Simple* and Professor Arno Peters, University of Bremen for the North-South map projection.

The Publishers would also like to thank the following for their permission to reproduce copyright photographs: Liverpool Daily Post & Echo: Cover; D.H.S.S./Controller Her Majesty's Stationery Office, Crown Copyright reserved: p 51; Máire Nic Suibhne: p 5; Tish Murtha: pp 8, 48; Mary Hay: p 11; Christian Aid/Sophie Baker: p 12; One Parent Families/Michael Abrahams: p 13; UNESCO: pp 15 (B Herzog), 72 (P Harrison); Daisy Hayes: pp 17, 25; John Twinning: pp 18, 71; Martin West: pp 20, 52; Eddie Parker: p 21; Camera Press: pp 23 (Vince Streano), 24 (Interfoto MTI + Hungary), 35; Family Planning Association/Donna Thynne: p 28; The Society for the Protection for Unborn Children/Donna Thynne: p 29; Barnabys Picture Library: p 30; Dr Barnardos: p 31; Colorific: p 32; Popperfoto: pp 33, 39, 83; Church Missionary Society: p 36; Child Poverty Action Group: p 37; The Corrymeela Community: p 40; International Voluntary Service: p 43; Daily Express: p 49; London Express News Service/Daily Star: p 54; Central Independent TV: p 55; The National Anti-Vivisection Society Ltd/Brian Gunn: p 56; Save the Children Fund/John Walmsley: p 59; The Metropolitan Police: p 60; Chr Kaiser Verlag, München: p 62; Associated Press: pp 63, 80; Illustrated London News: p 64; Youth and Education Department, Oxfam: pp 68, 69; NASA: p 74; Frank Herrmann/Sunday Times: p 76; World Health Organisation/I Guest: p 77; Hans Lachmann: p 87; The Samaritans: p 89.

Contents

To the Student 4
1 On Becoming a Person 5
2 The Family: Relationships 8
3 The Family: Structures 11
4 School 14
5 Friends and Neighbours 17
6 Sexual Love 20
7 Marriage 23
8 Divorce 26
9 The Human Embryo: Birth Control, Abortion 28
10 The Human Embryo: Infertility, Research 31
11 Prejudice and Human Rights 35
12 Work 42
13 Spare Time 45
14 Money 47
15 Addiction 50
16 Violence 54
17 Law and Punishment 57
18 Authority and Opposition 61
19 Service 66
20 War and Peace 69
21 The World Community 74
22 Suffering 79
23 Breaking Free 82
24 Fulfilment 85
25 Death and Eternity 88
Appendix: Summary of the Universal Declaration of Human Rights 91
Resources 92
Further Reading 94
Index of Biblical References 96

All quotations from the Bible are taken from the Revised Standard Version. Those from the Apocrypha are taken from the Jerusalem Bible.

To the Student

This book has been written for candidates sitting for any of the Christian Ethics or Christian Responsibility syllabuses at GCSE. Obviously a book which tried to cover every demand of these examinations in any detail would be far too long to publish. I have simply tackled each topic by setting down some basic facts, followed by ideas and questions so that you will be able to start thinking about these things for yourself. You will need to do further research into some of the issues which really interest you. For this purpose I have included a Resources section giving you the names and addresses of various societies that you may want to contact, and a list of books for further reading.

You will notice that many of the 'Over to you' questions relate to the Bible. All the examination syllabuses give a great many biblical references. I have tried to include as many of them as possible so that you will be able to study the relevant text.

I have not set any essays for written work because I think you will find it more useful if your teacher suggests essay topics from your board's papers.

If you look at the order of chapters you will see that I have followed the natural development of a person. We begin with ourselves, then the family. We move out to the school, friends and neighbours and other kinds of relationships, falling in love, perhaps marrying and having children. We learn to become part of a wider community and realise all the problems this brings. Some of the difficulties which are discussed may not come into your own experience but they concern all of us and need to be thought about. There are chapters on war and peace and the world community because today we are more aware than ever that we are world citizens as well as citizens of a particular country.

You will find that important terms, such as **Third World** and **nuclear family**, are printed in bold type and what they mean is explained in the text.

I hope you will enjoy working through this book and that it gets you thinking about things, discussing them and reading about them, so that you can come to your own conclusions.

1 On Becoming a Person

You are a human being – a person – which means, amongst other things, that you have a beginning and an end!

When you are young and you look into the future, it seems that you have a long time in front of you.

When you are old and you look back over your life, it can seem to have gone in a moment.

☐ Ask anyone you know who is over 70 years of age what they remember best about their life. What do they consider to be important in life, and why?

As a human being, therefore, the most important question you can ask yourself is:

> ☐ How can I make the best use of all my gifts and qualities, so that my life NOW is full and interesting?

If you find some worthwhile answers to the question, it can also mean that when you come to look back over the years, you will have the satisfaction of knowing you have had a good run for your money!

The purpose of this book

This book is aimed at setting out certain ideas to help you come to your own conclusions about many important matters. It is based on the belief that as a human being you have not only a physical body, a thinking department, feelings and emotions, but something else.

This something else is a kind of inner self which is distinctly you and no other. Sometimes it is called your soul or spirit. It responds to beauty, to wonder, to worship and to love.

> ☐ Do you know any poems or songs in which the words 'soul' or 'spirit' appear?

Many of the great religions of the world have tried to describe this essence. In the Old Testament, the writer of the first book, Genesis, says that men and women were made 'in the image of God'. We do not know precisely what he meant, but to believe that there is 'that of God' in yourself and in everyone else, adds up to a very special way of understanding human beings and what life is all about.

> ☐ Can you name five of the world's major religions? Do you know their places of origin?

God

We cannot prove or disprove the existence of God in the same way that we can prove our own or anyone's existence. But everywhere and at all times, men and women have believed in some kind of supernatural being or beings although they have called these beings by different names and have had different ideas about what God is like.

Jesus called God 'Father' (see p. 85) but when talking to a Samaritan woman at a well he clearly defined God as spirit (John 4:24). And the writer of 1 John, thinking deeply about the meaning of Jesus' life, came to the conclusion that God was Light and Love (1 John 1:5; 4:7–21). Down the centuries, people have felt God's spirit of truth and love, active in their lives.

Today scientific discoveries continually show us fresh facts about the marvellous world in which we live and the order of the whole universe. This has led a great many scientists and others to believe there must be a creative mind behind everything.

> ☐ Discuss these reasons for believing in the existence of God.

Necessary skills

If you wanted to become an athlete you would train your body to peak condition. If you had hopes of becoming an engineer or a home economics specialist you would study and develop the necessary skills.

The same applies to anything worthwhile in life that you want to do. It means hard work, concentrated effort and above all an understanding of what is required of you. You will probably need expert advice and training.

> ☐ What skills do you need for each of the following jobs: shop assistant, plumber, grave-digger, electrician, paper-deliverer, baby-minder, joiner, computer expert?

The skills you require in trying to perfect yourself as a human being are somewhat different. And of course people have a great variety of ideas not only about the way to do it but also about the end result. A lot depends upon the culture or society into which you were born. There are some people today who think that human beings are merely highly complicated machines. They do not accept that each person has an individual spirit or self with its own values. However, for the believer in God – to whatever religion he or she may belong – it is the imprint of God, or spark of God, which makes us distinct as human beings. The growth of this inner, spiritual self is all-important if we are to develop fully as people.

The human spirit

The spirit of a person expresses itself through thoughts, feelings, words and actions. Therefore everything we think, feel, say and do, matters. And if there is harmony and wholeness at the centre then there is every chance that this will spread to the rest of our lives.

Christian attitudes

The Christian believes that Jesus had a closer relationship with God than anyone else, either before or since his time. Many other people have been inspired by God, but the quality of Jesus' life was such that his immediate friends felt he was the Son of God in a very special way. He passed the acid test of actually living out what he taught, even though it meant that he came to a terrible end. The Christian therefore looks to Jesus as the expert in spiritual matters.

Jesus' teaching

As we discuss various issues, we shall look at any relevant piece of advice that Jesus gave his followers. We shall also look at any other biblical passage which might help us. It is important, however, that you think things through for yourself and discuss them with others. No one person knows all the answers.

Over to you

a) Look up Genesis 1:26–31. Remember this is *not* a scientific or historical account of Creation, because we simply do not know how it all began. The Priestly writers of this chapter were expressing their beliefs about human nature. Two points to notice – men and women were created at the same time. They were equally important. Together they completed one another, forming humanity.

Secondly, human beings were given power to rule, to reason and to make moral decisions but they were God's representatives because it is God's world. Therefore disaster would follow if they took actions which were contrary to God's will.

Discuss these ideas.

b) How long do you expect to live? How long do you want to live? Give your reasons for both answers.

c) Write out in your note books John 4:24 and 1 John 1:5; 4:16.

d) We use the word 'charisma' to talk about a person who has the power to inspire others. It comes from the Greek 'charis' which means grace. Used in a religious sense, it means a spiritual power given by God.

Which people today do you think have 'charisma' or are 'charismatic'?

Would you link their qualities in any way with God's spirit?

2 The Family: Relationships

- [ ] How much of a person is the baby you know best? Does the fact that the baby cannot talk properly make it less of a unique individual?

- [ ] Do you think that babies sometimes feel frustrated because they cannot express themselves fully, as for example when they have a pain?

Can you remember when you first became aware that you were a person? As you grow older this awareness of yourself becomes more insistent, so you cry or get angry, or smile and wheedle to get your own way. Even if you do not remember much of what it was like to be very young, perhaps you have a younger brother or sister or even a baby in the household.

Giving and receiving

The most important lesson we have to learn in the matter of growing up is that other people have needs and wants as well as we do. And the family is probably the best place in which to see that life is both a giving and a receiving. Jesus said that we must treat other people as we would like to be treated ourselves (Matthew 7:12). This sounds simple but in practice it is very hard. We have to learn to put ourselves in someone else's shoes. It is one thing for us to be greedy and pinch the best things from the dinner table; it is different if someone else does this and we are left with the second-best bits.

- [ ] What other examples can you think of where you would not like to receive the treatment you have given to another?

The generation gap

Difficulties arise when children grow older and feel that their parents do not understand them. Teenagers often feel there is an age gap between themselves and adults. You may know an older person who regularly irritates you by saying reprovingly, 'When I was your age I would not have dreamt of doing that ...' On the other hand young people may deliberately do something simply to shock their elders, not because they particularly want to take that action.

To feel rebellious is part of growing up. You feel you have to test out your ideas and opinions to find out what you really do think and believe. You also have to establish yourself as a person distinct from your family. But it is sad if rebellion takes the form of hurting or causing real pain to someone else. Where there is love, honesty and trust there is a chance that problems can be discussed and even sometimes solved.

> ☐ Discuss some of the differences between your generation and that of your parents, especially in the matter of dress, hairstyles, amusements.

Rebel without a cause (1950), starring James Dean, was the first film about teenage rebellion. What recent films deal with teenage rejection of adults?

> ☐ Do you think it is true that different generations find it hard to talk to each other? Is it because young people have a different way of expressing themselves or different lifestyle? What can be done to bridge any gap that might exist?

Parenthood

Parenthood is obviously a very responsible job. People have varying ideas about the most important qualities of a good parent.

> ☐ Put the following list in order, showing what you think are the most important qualities: steady and reliable; affectionate; considerate; disciplined; interested; even-tempered; strict; supportive; having a sense of humour; having some kind of religious faith; generous.

None of us are perfect, of course, but many qualities can come to people through experience and maturity.

> - ☐ Do you think we should take lessons in parenthood before becoming parents? Would you like to go to classes in learning how to be a parent and manage a home before you got married and had a child? What kind of arrangement would be helpful?
> - ☐ Would you expect there to be different advice for the boy and for the girl? Do you think both sexes should take an equal share in looking after children?

Sometimes parents forget that children are people who have deep feelings. They spoil them one minute and are harsh with them the next depending on their mood. And children have to learn that parents are people too, and parents may get tired, frustrated and unhappy.

> - ☐ Do you look at your parents simply as Mum and Dad or as people in their own right?

Jesus' teaching

Jesus was very clear in his teaching about children. He obviously loved them very much (Mark 9:36–7). He said they had a quality which adults ought to possess if they wanted to become citizens of the kingdom of God (Mark 10:14–15). He did not say specifically what this quality might be. He may have meant that children are usually eager and trustful. Perhaps he was talking about an openness, a ready willingness to learn, that it is easy to lose when one becomes an adult.

> - ☐ What do you think this quality might be?

Over to you

a) Look up Luke 2:41–52. This is the only story we have of Jesus as a boy. Although he was devoted to his parents, he put his responsibility to God first. Now read John 19:26–7. Even in his hour of agony, Jesus did not forget his mother and he put her in the care of his best friend.

Discuss Jesus' two approaches. Do you think they were contradictory? Could putting God first help you to care more for your parents? If so, in what way?

b) Look up Mark 7:9–13. Jesus is very angry with the scribes and Pharisees. He is obviously talking about an actual case. A son has ignored his parents' needs, pretending that he has dedicated all his money to God and therefore cannot support them. The Aramaic* word 'Corban' was used in the making of vows. The scribes thought that keeping the strict letter of the Law was more important sometimes than seeking out its true meaning and obeying its inner spirit (Exodus 20:12). Look up and write down in your notebook Exodus 20:12 and then, in your own words, say what it means to you.

*Aramaic – the language that Jesus and Palestinian Jews spoke in New Testament times.

c) Before the introduction of the Welfare State and the Old Age Pension, parents depended on their children to care for them when they became old. Now that we have pensions, old people's homes and other services, do you think families are less responsible than they ought to be in looking after aged relatives?

d) Look up Proverbs 13:24 and 22:6. Discuss the arguments that a good parent is a strict one and that what you learn as a child you never forget.

e) Look up Colossians 3:18–24. Remember that in Paul's day the man had absolute authority over his wife, his children and his slaves. Paul was revolutionary in proposing the idea that wives, children and slaves had some rights also.

Do you think all parents would agree with the view that they should not 'provoke' their children?

f) In Malachi 2:10, the Old Testament writer sees God as the father and creator of his children. Jesus put special emphasis on this belief and taught his disciples to pray to God as Father (Matthew 6:9). Look up these passages and write down Malachi 2:10 in your notebooks.

Also look up Matthew 7:9–12 where Jesus shows God's love for humanity by comparing God's attitude with the natural behaviour of any affectionate human father.

3 The Family: Structures

If you and I had been born two hundred years ago, we should probably have lived in a village in the country where everyone knew everyone else and we all belonged to one of several large families. The fathers of these families would either have worked on the land or as servants on a large estate. With the invention of machinery, new industries sprang up and families moved into towns to look for jobs. The small family group of father, mother and children then lived separately from the grandparents, uncles, aunts and cousins. This smaller unit of two generations is known as the **nuclear family**. Today it is the typical family group in the Western world.

In this century, improved medical care and birth control meant that couples could decide how many children they might have, knowing that those were likely to survive. The smaller family needed smaller accommodation and became better off.

A nuclear family.

☐ How many brothers and sisters, living grandparents, uncles, aunts and cousins do you have? How often do you see them? How many relations can you number with whom you keep in touch? How does it compare with the families of your friends and classmates at school?

The nuclear family has been seen as the basic unit of society. A great deal of advertising aims at encouraging people to buy lovely homes, fit them up with the latest labour-saving gadgets, decorate them with beautiful furnishings and so on. Other advertisers sell all kinds of food for the family and its pets, or games for the children.

☐ How many television advertisements that you see regularly are aimed at improving the lifestyle of the nuclear family? Keep a list of these for one complete week and compare your numbers with your friends.

Different kinds of family groupings

There are great changes taking place in our society. Recent research suggests that only 44 per cent of the population in England and Wales now live in a nuclear family. Here are some of the terms given to other types of community life:

Extended family

This is the larger grouping of blood relatives and those who have come into the family by marriage. The extended family was the most common unit in previous generations and is still so in many countries, such as India and Pakistan.

Expanded family

This is the term used for people who have decided to live together, some of whom are not related by blood. For example two Christian ministers and their wives and children might share a large house and live together as a family. Someone whose home is too big might take in students so that during term time they all live together and share the household duties. The mentally handicapped, the elderly or other people in need, are often cared for in a large house or community. This means that a family atmosphere can be created.

Reconstituted family

This consists of step-parents and step-brothers and sisters. When divorcees remarry, the children of the first marriage become part of the reconstituted family. One of the partners is a divorced person in one out of nine new marriages today.

One-parent family

One in eight children (well over a million) in Britain now live with one parent only. These single parents may have been widowed, divorced or deserted by their partners. In some cases the parent is a single woman who, for one reason or another, has not married the father of the child.

Some of these single parents live with their own parents or relatives. If the mother goes out to work, the grandmother may possibly look after the child. Some single parents remarry and thus form reconstituted families. Others manage entirely on their own. Life can be very hard and difficult, however, for these families and often they are very poor.

An extended family, grandmother, mother and daughter, are seen working together in India. British people of Asian origin often keep the extended family unit. How much do you see of your own extended family?

Fathers head 12 per cent of one-parent families.

☐ Discuss what problems might arise from these different family groupings. There might be jealousy, for example, within the reconstituted family.

Single people

A quarter of the population consists of single people who are not living in any kind of family group. They could be young, middle-aged, elderly, unmarried, divorced, or widowed people. They also include people who are actually living together (**co-habiting**) but who are not married. Once such a relationship has lasted long enough to be considered permanent, the law accepts it as a **common law marriage**.

Christian attitudes

In Jesus' day the extended family was the normal pattern in Jewish life. The family itself has always been of central importance to both Jew and Christian. However, Jesus could see limitations within the family. He showed that he thought it should be broadened in its outlook (Mark 3:31–5). He believed that the family really found its fulfilment in being part of a larger community (Mark 10:29–31).

☐ What do you expect from your family?

☐ Do you think blood relations are all-important? Do you expect your friends to give you the same kind of love and support as your close relatives?

Loneliness can be a great problem to those people who do not feel that they are important or that they belong to others. Christians see everyone as part of the expanded family of the human race. Everyone matters, whatever their sex, age, race or social status.

Over to you

a) Write down the different terms which are used for family groupings, with examples for each kind.

Discuss what can be done to help people who are lonely.

b) Read Mark 3:31–5. Jesus' mother and brothers came to visit him while he was on a teaching tour. When he heard of their arrival he asked the crowd, 'Who are my mother and my brothers?' and then answered the question himself: 'Whoever does the will of God is my brother, and sister, and mother.'

Do you think he was being unkind to his family? Discuss what his family might have thought about this and what the crowd thought.

What lesson was he teaching?

c) Read Mark 10:29–31. Jesus was discussing the many hardships his disciples might go through, including giving up their families for the sake of the kingdom of God. He talked about the great family of believers to which they would belong. This would give them the love and support they needed.

What modern examples can you think of where someone who loved his or her family might put them in second place to their job or commitment?

What lesson was Jesus teaching?

d) Write a project on the problems which one-parent families face. Discuss what support can be given to them.

4 School

There are some who believe that the purpose of school is to help young people become good citizens so that they support and contribute to the welfare of society as a whole. Other educationalists believe that the individual is all-important and that the school must help each boy and girl to develop personal potential to the full. These experts say it is no good supplying children with lots of facts and figures in which they are not particularly interested. The teacher must start with the children's own concern and go on from there. This is known as **child-centred education**. Of course, most schools try to combine both these ideas. But truly child-centred learning would require many more teachers than are at present available. At least in Britain we are lucky because everyone has to go to school by law and the state pays for 96 per cent of the cost. In many poor countries there are not enough schools and millions of people cannot even read or write.

The purpose of school

Here are some suggestions as to what school may do for you:

1 Help you to pass examinations which could lead to a good job.

2 Develop skills in vocational subjects, such as in typing or woodwork, so that you can go on to further training after school. This will also help you later to get a good job.

3 Develop your ability to express yourself both orally and on paper so that you will be able to stand up for your rights when necessary.

4 Open your eyes to the history of things and people and to all kinds of ideas and interests, such as in the study of art, or literature, or the world of nature, or science.

5 Teach you how to accept authority and learn discipline. These qualities are needed in the adult world whether at work or in the home.

6 Help you to live in a wider community than the home and to take responsibility for others as well as for yourself. When we see and appreciate the great differences that exist between people, we find plenty of scope for making good friends.

- [ ] Put these six points in order of importance as you see them. Give your reasons.
- [ ] Do you disagree with any of them? What other suggestions could be added?
- [ ] Why do you think that some boys and girls so hate school that they regularly play truant?

Religious education

Sometimes this subject is taught very badly in school and students get bored. But in many schools the R.E. teacher sees and believes that his/her role is very important because as human beings we have this inner core, or spirit, that should be given an opportunity to grow and develop. The great religions of the world have always seen religious education as essential

Peruvian Uru Indians learning to read. While some pupils in rich countries play truant from school, people in less developed areas of the world will put up with great difficulties and hardship for the sake of gaining a very basic education.

because it leads on to a proper understanding of what life is all about.

☐ What reasons can you give to support this view?

Jesus as a teacher

Jesus was a great teacher. Wherever he went large crowds followed him to listen to his words. He usually told them stories which made them think and see things from a different perspective. He used very familiar situations to help people understand what he was teaching them. For example, in Luke 15:11–32 he pictured God as a loving father. In the story it is the father's love which in the end helps the younger son to change his ways and come home. The elder brother's attitude is very different. He despises his brother and resents his father's generosity.

> ☐ Read this story for yourself. Discuss the crowd's reaction to it. Imagine there were listeners like the two sons and parents who were disappointed in their children. What lessons would they learn? What makes the story-method of teaching effective?

The learning process

The purpose of education is hotly debated among teachers as well as pupils. And teachers need to see their pupils as individual people, just as much as pupils need to realise that teachers are people and are not simply symbols of authority or repression. The teacher's expertise is there for the benefit of the pupil. This is the whole learning process. Where mutual respect and encouragement flourish, both teacher and pupil are satisfied.

The wise sage of Ecclesiasticus said that one should never stop learning (6:18):

> My son, from your earliest youth choose instruction, and till your hair is white you will keep finding wisdom!

> ☐ What kind of 'instruction' and 'wisdom' was he talking about? Do you agree with him?
>
> ☐ Do you consider that you are getting the most out of your school experience and giving all you can to it?
>
> ☐ If you could change things in your school, what would you do not only for your own benefit but for everyone else?

Over to you

a) Read Mark 4:1–9. This gives a good picture of Jesus as a teacher. Perhaps he was sitting in his boat on the Lake and actually saw a man sowing seed on the hillside. In the story the soil represents the different ways in which people received Jesus' teaching (the seed). Some were too hard or too shallow or too busy with other things to take it in. But where people received what he had to say gladly, their whole lives became different and they passed on the 'good news' to others. We all of us respond differently to what we hear or see, what we are told or shown, whether it is a television programme or a lesson in school. We may learn facts to pass an examination, then forget them quickly. This shallow impact is very different from the deep impression which can last a lifetime.

Discuss the different kinds of responses to 'education' in all its forms. Would you say that you remember a story or an experience better than a fact?

b) Find out how many people in this country leave school unable to read or write. How is it that many of them are able to learn these skills when they go to adult classes? What do you think could have gone wrong at school?

c) Look at the question about truancy above. What difficulties can arise if teenagers do not finish their education satisfactorily?

Can you suggest any possible answers to this problem in our society?

5 Friends and Neighbours

One of the most interesting things about growing up is that we become more able to learn about others. Life becomes exciting when we realise how many other people there are to meet, people with whom we can have worthwhile relationships.

The value of friendship

Jesus called his disciples his friends and told them to love each other even as he had loved them. When he knew he was going to die he said (John 15:13):

> 'Greater love has no man than this, that a man lay down his life for his friends.'

Willingness to sacrifice oneself for a friend is an extreme example of the kind of love, trust and loyalty which can exist in a group of people who are all united in a common cause or to a specific leader. Here are two more sayings about friendship (Proverbs 18:24; Ecclesiasticus 6:17):

> There are friends who pretend to be friends, but there is a friend who sticks closer than a brother.

> Whoever fears the Lord makes true friends, for as a man is, so is his friend.

- ☐ Do you think it is always true that we are attracted to people like ourselves?
- ☐ What qualities would you expect to find in a friend and what would you be prepared to give in return?

Conflict

Even among the best of friends arguments and difficulties arise. In the small and struggling early Christian communities it was essential that conflicts should be quickly resolved. So a code of practice was laid down (Matthew 18:15–20). Every effort to make up the quarrel should be made by the two people involved. The longer we delay our attempts at reconciliation, the harder it becomes to admit our fault and to be prepared to forgive. Paul said (Ephesians 4:26):

> Do not let the sun go down on your anger.

- [ ] Jealousy, pride, temper, lying, flattery, disloyalty, selfishness, can all cause disagreement between friends. Put them in order of seriousness, giving your reasons.

Old and young can enjoy one another's friendship, each gaining from the other.

- [ ] Are there some things which would make you finish the friendship even if you forgave the person?

Who is my neighbour?

A lawyer asked Jesus this question after Jesus had agreed with his summary of the law (taken from Deuteronomy 6:4–5 and Leviticus 19:18). The lawyer probably thought his neighbour was a fellow Jew but he wanted to be sure. Jesus replied with a story which makes it plain that the compassionate person sees anyone in need as a neighbour, regardless of race or social status. (The whole account is in Luke 10:25–37.)

- [ ] Understandably, people may feel they do not want to become involved in someone else's trouble, but would you agree that we need each other in times of stress?

> ☐ Think of examples (an accident, death or illness, for instance) where good neighbours can be an invaluable help.

Any very selfish person becomes isolated and is therefore only half alive because he/she sees only him or herself and no other. As we live in a modern welfare state, it is perhaps easy to think that the state will take care of everything but it is a mistaken idea. We need our families, our friends and our neighbours and they need us. And it is in learning to share, to take responsibility and to work with others that we grow and develop as people.

> ☐ Do you think it is possible to be friends with one's parents or grandparents, or does the generation gap prevent this?
>
> ☐ Is it easier to be friends with people of the same sex as oneself than with the opposite sex? Should this be so?
>
> ☐ Do you think it is difficult to be friends with someone who has more money than you, or is of a different religion or a different colour?
>
> ☐ Can people with different educational backgrounds be friends?
>
> ☐ Can patients and nurses, or teachers and pupils, or lawyers and clients be friends? What might prevent friendship in these cases? Is it wise to mix business with pleasure?

Forgiveness

Jesus said it was no use going to worship God if you were not first at one with your neighbour (Matthew 5:23–4). The chief characteristic of all his teaching was that we should forgive both friends *and* enemies (Mark 11:25; Matthew 5:7, 43–8). But we can only forgive those who hurt or harm us if we see them as individuals worthy of consideration and understanding. When we think of 'the Enemy' we may see only a masked being who is frightening and dangerous. We forget that even enemies are real people in their own right.

> ☐ Would you consider it weakness to forgive? Can you forgive and still punish?

Over to you

a) Look up Luke 10:25–37. Act or role play the story, thinking of a modern equivalent to the situation. Remember that the Samaritan was a despised half-caste but he understood what Leviticus 19:18 was all about – much better than the professional lawyer and priest. The priest and Levite would not want to make themselves ritually unclean* by contact with blood or the dead, especially if they were on their way to a Temple Service. Note how they emphasised the letter or outward form of the Law rather than its inner spirit.

*ritually unclean – unfit to take part in a religious service.

b) Read the letter of Paul to his friend Philemon. Paul had helped Onesimus, a runaway slave, who had now become a Christian. Paul feels he must send him back to his master but he begs Philemon to forgive Onesimus for running away and to treat him now as a brother.

In the first century AD such an action would be unheard of, but the fact that the letter is preserved confirms that Philemon did as Paul asked him. Tradition says Onesimus went on to become a bishop. Discuss this story in the light of Jesus' teaching in Matthew 5:38–42.

c) Read Ruth chapter 1, a story of love and friendship between an Israelite woman and her Moabite daughter-in-law. Discuss verses 16 and 17 in view of the questions and discussion topics in this chapter.

d) Look up Ecclesiasticus 6:14–17 where the sage talks about the qualities of a faithful friend. Write down what qualities you most value in your friends.

e) Look back over the whole of this chapter and then write down your answer to the question, 'Who is my neighbour?'

6 Sexual Love

The English word *love* covers a wide range of emotions. If we had been Greek-speaking Christians in the New Testament period we would have used the word 'agape' for the love which existed between people in the Christian community and the word 'eros' for sexual love. To help distinguish between the different kinds of loving, we often use the phrase 'to fall in love' when we are talking about sexual attraction.

People can attract us because of the way they look, or talk, or think, or because they seem to like us and want to be in our company. Sexual attraction is a normal and natural process which comes through the awakening of sexual feelings and the desire to express these feelings in touching, kissing and caressing the other person. At their deepest level, sexual feelings can lead to the act of physical union, which sexual intercourse brings about.

We should not take the sexual side of our natures lightly. Nor should we consider sexual feeling shameful. It is mistaken to call it the 'beast' in us as opposed to the 'angel' or spirit. Our sexual nature must be used as an opportunity both to give and receive love and to bring children who are loved and wanted into the world.

We have to understand clearly, however, that sexual attraction does not automatically lead to sexual loving, just as any first attraction does not necessarily lead to a deep friendship.

> ☐ Do you think it would be a good idea if we had a separate word for each different aspect of love? How many different words can you think of which express family feeling; friendship; concern for others; sexual attraction?

Sex in our society

We live in a society which downgrades the value of sexual loving and which wrongly uses sex to make money. Sex is used to make people buy certain goods. It is always a standby in a comedian's small talk to get a laugh. It has even become fashionable in certain sections of the entertainment industry to show the more brutal aspect of sexual behaviour, such as rape and cruelty. There are different categories of 'blue' films, video 'nasties' and of **pornography** – the word used to describe the treatment of **obscene** or indecent subjects in the arts or entertainment. But one thing they all have in common, although to a greater or lesser degree, is that they debase human beings. They show human beings acting in an unnatural or horrible way.

Ordinary people do not enjoy hurting others. We are capable of being tender and sympathetic. We try to learn self-control for the sake of ourselves and other people. We know how to be faithful, loving and considerate. These basic good qualities are far more typical of human beings than their opposites. If it were not so, we should have destroyed our species long ago.

> ☐ As a teenager, what is your opinion of the fact that video 'nasties' are now being shown to children under ten? How will this affect their views of grown-up behaviour?
>
> ☐ Look at any advertisement which uses sex to sell its product. Discuss whether or not this kind of advertising influences people's attitudes to sexual love.

Sexual equality

Sexual attraction, of course, has always been strongly present. But in previous centuries men and women have looked at their relationship with each other from rather different standpoints. The man regarded the woman as his possession and she in turn could be very dependent on him. Birth control methods were not easily available so sexual intercourse could often result in pregnancy. If unmarried, the woman would then be disgraced. Both she and her child could be turned out of her family and suffer great hardship. On the other hand, a woman who became a wife would probably have to bear many children and would need total support from her husband.

In this century, women have fought not only for social and financial independence but for some degree of sexual freedom as well. This has been made possible by modern methods of birth control. There is now a far greater degree of equality in men and women's sexual relationships as well as in their ordinary lives. This equality does not mean that people are necessarily more promiscuous, i.e. have sex with many different people without careful choice. The vast majority choose to express their freedom in entering into responsible and loving partnerships.

> ☐ In spite of the social changes which have happened, do boys and girls still have different attitudes towards sex? If so, why do you think this is?
>
> ☐ Do you think men and women are sexually equal? Give reasons to support your views.

Homosexuality

A **homosexual** is sexually attracted to someone of his or her own sex, unlike the majority of people who are **heterosexual** (attracted to someone of the opposite sex). In previous centuries a man accused of sexual relations with another man faced the death sentence under UK law. Even in

Homosexuality can now be shown more openly in the media. This award-winning film also focuses on other things.

the 1960s, homosexual acts were 'crimes' leading to prison sentences and public disgrace.

Scientific research shows that we all have both male and female genes. Sometimes the homosexual genetic balance is slightly different from the usual one. Perhaps 10 per cent of the population is naturally homosexual. The present UK laws aim to protect young people from all sexual abuse, whether heterosexual or homosexual. But adults are now free to enter into private homosexual relationships. Some branches of the Christian church still condemn homosexuality as a sinful perversion of God's creation. They teach that the person concerned should try to change his/her sexual nature and certainly never express it in a physical relationship. On the other hand, many of the Christian denominations have homosexual societies and some practising Christians openly say they are homosexual and that this does not conflict with their faith. They enter into deep and permanent relationships on the basis of mutual love and trust.

Christian attitudes

Although Christians have different ideas about some aspects of sexual behaviour, they would all agree on one basic principle. We all have a divine spark in us which gives every human being a certain kind of dignity. Therefore we need to treat each other with mutual respect and consideration. We also need to value ourselves properly.

The sexual side of our natures is a necessary part of our personality. At best, human beings have sexual intercourse to express their deep love for one another and their feeling of union. They do not choose to have intercourse merely so as to produce children. All Christians would agree that sexual desire must be expressed through love not lust. Love is just as intense and passionate as lust, but is quite a different matter. It depends on how we regard the other person. Do we see the other as an object which will satisfy our immediate desire? Or as a person in his/her own right to be respected, considered, cherished and cared for?

Over to you

a) Look up Genesis 2:21–5. This is part of the ancient Hebrew myth of creation. In it the writer is explaining through picture language how he believes that woman is man's ideal companion in all things. When the man sees her he is overjoyed at finding his true mate at last.

Perhaps the writer is also trying to explain sexual desire. He says that as man and woman were originally one flesh, so they long to become one again and through their sexual union they are able to produce a child. The writer is of course a man of his time and he therefore places the woman under the man's authority, saying that the man names her. On the other hand he also sees sexual union and marriage as natural and right – part of God's creation. Do people still believe that woman is under man's authority, in spite of women's fight for equality?

b) Look up Mark 9:42–9. Jesus is using poetic language so we must not take his words literally. He is speaking out strongly against those who cause others harm or who lead astray people who are less experienced than themselves. We must practise discipline, self-control and even self-denial not only for the sake of others but for our own good. We may find that we have to give up the chance of immediate satisfaction or pleasure for the sake of the long-term benefit. We have to choose between living creatively or destructively.

We should not take the picture of hell fire literally to mean eternal damnation. It is a way of saying that someone can cease to be a person if he/she destroys him or herself by living wrongly.

What do you understand by hell?
When is self-denial necessary?

c) Look up 1 Corinthians 13; write down verses 4–7. Some people believe that Paul had Jesus in mind when he wrote these famous words. They have been taken to express the Christian ideal of love, however it expresses itself.

What modern examples can you give of people who come close to this ideal?

d) Make a short list of advertisements which use sex to sell their products. Write a different advertisement for any one of these, leaving out the sexual appeal, but showing the real value of the goods on sale.

e) Write down the one basic *principle* about sexual behaviour on which all Christians would agree.

7 Marriage

- ☐ Do you plan to marry when you are older?
- ☐ Do you think marriage is a good thing?
- ☐ List some of the qualities you would consider essential in a successful partnership.

The vast majority of Christians believe that people should only have sexual intercourse within a *permanent* relationship. In a secure, permanent relationship sexual love has a chance to grow and deepen.

For centuries the Christian Church has taught that this permanent relationship is marriage. And its idea of marriage is based on the teaching of Jesus in Mark 10:1–12. Although Jesus is asked a question on divorce, he answers with his own views on marriage. Quoting from Genesis 1:27 and 2:24, he stresses that any real marriage is based on the principle of unity between two people. Through sexual intercourse, two separate individuals can become one. Their physical union shows that they are totally committed to one another. Their relationship should be permanent and it should take first place over all others. Jesus was very far ahead of his time because he talked of men and women as equals in marriage, and even in divorce, as his later comment on this issue shows.

Legal marriage in most countries is monogamous (one husband, one wife). The Mormon sect allows illegal polygamy (one husband, several wives). How would polygamy prevent men and women from having an equal relationship?

- ☐ How important is it that men and women should be regarded as equal? Should men and women each take an equal share of responsibility for the home and the children?

- ☐ Can marriage work if wife and husband reverse their traditional roles? A woman who is earning a good salary might return to work after she has had her child, while the man stays at home to look after the family. Do you think this is a good idea?

- ☐ A man's wife may die tragically young, or desert him, or fall very ill and become an invalid; do you know of cases where the father has given up his job to care for his children for these or similar reasons?

A minority of Christians accept the fact that some young people nowadays prefer to live together for a time before they make a final decision about getting married. This may be because they have high standards of marriage and want their own to last. They do not want to make mistakes at the very beginning. And they are not at all casual in their sexual relationships.

> ☐ Do you think living together might be a good preparation for marriage? Or do you think that such an uncertain future for the relationship might place a strain on both partners?

The marriage ceremony

If you look at any of the forms of marriage service used by the main Christian denominations,* you will find that in all of them the couple take a vow or promise to be faithful to each other before God and in front of their families and friends. The solemn promise to stand by each other in all times of hardship, sickness, trials and old age makes marriage different from any other relationship. It emphasises the *moral* nature of marriage. It is based on the belief that each one of us is a whole person with an inner or spiritual self as well as a physical body. It is the spiritual self which ought to control and guide us.

denominations – separate Christian Churches, e.g. Methodist, Church of England, Baptist, Roman Catholic, United Reformed.

> ☐ Obviously parents feel committed to love and look after their children and children may care for their parents as they get old. Brothers and sisters may also take on responsibilities for each other. But in what sense is the marriage contract different from these other family relationships?

Here is an extract from the Church of England marriage service:

The bride and bridegroom stand before the priest, and the priest says:

We have come together in the presence of God, to witness the marriage of N and N, to ask his

The joining of man and wife in a Roman Catholic wedding ceremony in Hungary.

blessing on them, and to share in their joy. Our Lord Jesus Christ was himself a guest at a wedding in Cana of Galilee, and through his Spirit he is with us now.

The Scriptures teach us that marriage is a gift of God in creation and a means of his grace, a holy mystery in which man and woman become one flesh. It is God's purpose that, as husband and wife give themselves to each other in love throughout their lives, they shall be united in that love as Christ is united with his Church.

Marriage is given, that husband and wife may comfort and help each other, living faithfully together in need and in plenty, in sorrow and in joy. It is given, that with delight and tenderness they may know each other in love, and, through the joy of their bodily union, may strengthen the union of their hearts and lives. It is given, that they may have children and be blessed in caring for them and bringing them up in accordance with God's will, to his praise and glory.

In marriage husband and wife belong to one another, and they begin a new life together in the community. It is a way of life that all should honour; and it must not be undertaken carelessly, lightly, or selfishly, but reverently, responsibly, and after serious thought.

This is the way of life, created and hallowed by God, that N and N are now to begin. They will each give their consent to the other; they will join hands

A registry office wedding. In what ways is this different from a church wedding? Why is it called 'a civil ceremony'?

and exchange solemn vows, and in token of this they will give and receive a ring.

Therefore, on this their wedding day we pray with them, that, strengthened and guided by God, they may fulfil his purpose for the whole of their earthly life together.

> ☐ What does this extract say are the three purposes of marriage? Discuss these and any other points arising from the extract.

Children

Research has shown that a child needs a stable background until it has grown up sufficiently to make its own way in life.

One expert has suggested that there might be two kinds of marriage. The first would be for the couple who intend to have children. They would promise to stay together for at least 15 years and until the children are old enough to cope with any possible breakup of the home. The second type of marriage would be for the couple who wish to share their lives with one another but who do not want to have children. They would have more freedom to end the marriage by mutual consent if they found the relationship was not successful.

> ☐ What do you think of these ideas?

Christian attitudes

The Christian believes, however, that in a true marriage two people are permanently and lovingly involved with each other, whatever difficult and joyful circumstances they meet together during their lives. And they need to look outward to others as well as to themselves, if their love is to grow and mature.

Over to you

a) The books of the Old Testament come from a very different cultural background from our own. Ancient Hebrews believed that every girl must be a virgin at her marriage, and she must remain completely faithful to her husband afterwards. She was her husband's possession and the mother of his children. Nevertheless she could be loved, admired and revered.

Read Proverbs 31:10–31 to see what portrait the Hebrew sage paints of the ideal wife. Discuss your reactions to this picture, both from the male and female point of view.

b) Read Ephesians 5:21–33 and Colossians 3:18–19. You will see that Paul also was a man of his time. In other words, he assumed that the man had full authority over his family, because he was a husband, father and master. But you will also note how enlightened Paul was. In spite of the world around him, he saw that the woman should have some rights – list what they were. He compared marriage to the relationship between Christ and his Church. What does this tell us about the value he set on marriage?

c) Jesus himself was a Jew, brought up in the Jewish religion and traditions. What would be revolutionary and amazing to his people about his views on sexual matters?

d) Look at the topics for discussion on p. 23 about equality and roles. Try to find out how modern couples share responsibilities and even change roles according to circumstances.

8 Divorce

During the last 50 years divorce has become more and more common. There are many reasons why marriages break down and why there are more divorces. Here are some:

1 People are unrealistic about marriage and expect too much from it. They see it as one way of being fulfilled and finding security, but when poverty, hardship, ill health or other problems arise, these cause great strains on the relationship.
2 Divorce is now much easier and the shame of divorce has been removed, so partners might not try so hard to keep the marriage going.
3 Partners marry too early, when both are too young to know either themselves or each other really well.
4 They have children too soon after marriage. This may cause strain and tension if neither partner is prepared for parenthood.
5 The woman wants to keep working and does not want to give it up to have children or to take charge of running the home, whereas the man wants her to do both these things.
6 A woman can now be financially independent and therefore if a marriage is unsatisfactory she no longer has to stay with her husband just because of money.
7 People are living longer, healthier lives. In earlier times many second marriages took place after the death of a partner; now that people are living longer, divorce is necessary to allow a second marriage.

According to recent statistics (1984–5), one in three marriages (34 per cent) now ends in divorce.

At the present time the only accepted reason for divorce for either party is that the marriage has *irretrievably* broken down. In support of this the person seeking divorce can claim **adultery** (i.e. sexual intercourse between the partner and someone other than the husband or wife), **unreasonable behaviour** (e.g. mental or physical cruelty, insanity), or **desertion** for a continuous period of at least two years.

If both parties consent, a divorce may be granted if the couple have lived apart for a continuous period of two years. If one party refuses consent, then the couple must have lived apart for a continuous period of at least five years for divorce to be allowed. It is also at present illegal to seek a divorce within one year of marriage except in cases of extreme hardship.

The Law decides the financial arrangements between the couple, especially where children are involved. The 1984 Divorce Reform Act brought in the 'clean break' order, which means that the husband (except in certain circumstances) need not give his wife any financial support (**maintenance**) from the time of the break in the marriage, or in the future.

> ☐ Statistics show that the younger you are when you get married the less likely it is that your marriage will last. Why do you think this might be?

Although divorce is now much easier, suffering and hardship are still present. A father may not be allowed to see his children. A divorced mother may earn much less than her ex-husband and find it very hard to support the family. The children may feel torn apart by the split up of their parents' marriage. These are only three of the many ways in which people may suffer through divorce.

Unfortunately many people do not realise that there are organisations which can offer advice on their problems. They can help when marriages go through difficult patches, so that some breakdowns can be avoided. The National Marriage Guidance Council and the Catholic Marriage Advisory Service are two of them.

> ☐ Discuss some of the ways in which both parents and children might suffer if a marriage breaks up.

Jesus' teaching

According to Jewish law a man could divorce his wife if he found 'some indecency in her' (Deuteronomy 24:1–4). A woman had no legal rights at all. In Jesus' day, two famous rabbis disagreed about what 'some indecency' meant. One said it meant being sexually unfaithful, while the other said it was failure in the woman's running of her home.

Jesus and Paul lived in societies where the woman and her children were totally dependent on the man. They were therefore very much aware that the divorced woman could be left without any means of supporting herself.

Jesus emphasised the true nature of marriage. He warned that lust can often cause a marriage to break down and (according to Matthew 5:32) said that the only acceptable cause for divorce was sexual unfaithfulness. Paul condemned divorce (1 Corinthians 7:10–11) but did agree with separation under certain circumstances (7:12–16).

> ☐ When the parents violently disagree, do you think it is better for the children if the family stays together, or should the parents part and perhaps eventually remarry?

Christian attitudes

For centuries the Christian Church has taught that sexual intercourse belongs only within marriage and that marriage can only be dissolved by the death of one of the partners. However, many Christians today recognise that if people are neglected, exploited, or cruelly misused by their partner, they should be able to seek divorce.

The Roman Catholic Church however does not accept divorce, but will **annul** a marriage (i.e. state that it was never a real marriage) under special circumstances.

The Anglican Church will only permit remarriage of divorced people in church if their bishop gives his consent to it. The Free Churches are less strict in this matter. But all Christians would say that marriage is a **sacrament** (that is, an important religious ceremony which is also a sign of inner blessing) and must be taken very seriously. The partners must really intend to enter into a life-long relationship.

■■■■■■■■■■■■■■■■■■■■■■■■■■■
Over to you

a) Read John 7:53–8:11. The family unit was so important in Jewish eyes that adultery was punishable by death (Deuteronomy 22:22–4). This fact lies behind the story told in John 7:53–8:11, although it is not certain that the Jewish authorities could legally put anyone to death in Jesus' day. Discuss Jesus' attitude.

b) Look up the biblical passages mentioned above, i.e. Matthew 5:32, 1 Corinthians 7:10–11, 12–16. Notice how both Jesus and Paul raised the level of men's thinking about women.

c) Some experts say it is a mistake to rush into a second marriage too soon after the first marriage breaks down. If people have not come to grips with the reasons why the first marriage failed, they will take unsolved problems into the second marriage, causing that to fail too. Discuss these views.

d) Invite someone from the National Marriage Guidance Council or another similar body to come to school and talk about how couples can be helped to resolve some of their problems.

e) Write out the reasons why marriages may break down from p. 26, putting them in order of importance. Say what you think about each.

■■■■■■■■■■■■■■■■■■■■■■■■■■■

9 The Human Embryo:
Birth control, Abortion

Today, because of medical and scientific research, we know far more about the beginnings of human life than any preceding generation. Many feminists and others now maintain that a woman has the right to decide whether she will bear a child or not. Three things make this possible:

1 Modern methods of birth control (**contraception**).

2 **Abortion** is now legal in certain well-defined circumstances.

3 There are various methods of producing a child for an **infertile** (childless) couple.

Birth control

Contraceptives are easily available. In theory this means that no child should be born who is not wanted or planned. In practice, however, many women do become unexpectedly pregnant, either through ignorance, mistake or the fact that contraceptives are not always reliable.

The Roman Catholic Church teaches that any 'artificial' method of birth control is against the law of God. According to this belief, married people who wish to limit their family should practise self-control. This means that they must only have sexual intercourse at 'safe' periods in the menstrual cycle. The present Pope stands firm on this traditional teaching. He sees the health and well-being of the nuclear family as central to the good of society.

In the main, the Protestant Churches agree with the use of modern contraceptives. They believe that Jesus considered intercourse within marriage as an act of union between two people; he did not insist that sex was only for the purpose of having children.

> ☐ Thousands of teenage girls start unwanted pregnancies each year. Why do you think this is so? Do you think there is enough discussion of birth control matters and sex education both for girls and boys at school or in the home?
>
> ☐ Should sex education be left entirely to parents, since it is their personal responsibility?

There are 8 methods of birth control

This isn't one of them

Find out more about family planning from your family doctor, any family planning clinic, Brook Advisory Centre or the Family Planning Information Service.

fpa

Abortion

An abortion is when a pregnancy is ended before a baby capable of surviving on its own outside the mother's body is born. An abortion can either happen naturally, i.e. a miscarriage, or it can be induced, i.e. done deliberately. Any girl or woman can now consider having an abortion if she finds she has become pregnant against her wishes. Under the terms of the 1967 Abortion Act, a doctor may legally prescribe an abortion if he/she and another doctor feel there is a risk to the life of the pregnant woman, or her physical and mental health, or that of her children. The doctors may also prescribe abortion if there is a substantial risk that the child would be seriously handicapped by physical or mental abnormality. The Act leaves a great deal of judgement to the doctors.

Anti-abortionists

Among both Christians and others, there is a strong movement which believes that the unborn child must be protected by law, since it has no way to protect itself. Many anti-abortionists believe that the child comes into being at the time it is *conceived*, therefore to remove the foetus is murder. They also claim that it is impossible to know what an individual will be worth. Thousands of unwanted and even seriously unhealthy children have made supreme contributions to society.

Pro-abortionists

Their argument rests on two beliefs. First that a woman has the right to decide whether she will have a child. Second that the human foetus, although potentially a human being, is not actually so until *28 weeks old*. This latter point raises all sorts of difficulties as some doctors believe that there should be no abortions after 24 weeks and others want an even shorter time limit.

The medical view

On the whole, medical opinion believes that legalised abortion is a lesser evil than the horrors of illegal back-street operations by unqualified people. In the recent past these often caused the patient's death or permanent injury.

This poster is part of the anti-abortion campaign by The Society for the Protection of Unborn Children. Can it be criticised for being too emotional?

Christian attitudes

All Christians would agree that to use abortion as a means of birth control is evil, but not all would condemn its legalisation.

Roman Catholics denounce abortion altogether. They believe that the foetus is an individual human being from the beginning.

On the other hand many Protestants believe that the embryo should be protected from the start, but not if it endangers the life of its mother. It is also argued that a woman who is forced into unwanted pregnancy through seduction and rape should be allowed abortion. This

Women march to demand the right to decide about abortion for themselves. Is the mother the only person whose opinion on this matter needs to be heard?

would lessen her suffering and would not necessarily debase human life.

Christians stress, however, that throughout society we need a much more responsible attitude towards sexual relationships. At its best, sexual love expresses one person's total commitment to another. The outcome of that commitment may be a third person, the unborn child. This possibility is something for which *both* the man and the woman are completely responsible.

☐ What are your views on the subject of abortion?

Over to you

a) Old and New Testament writers look on the birth of a child as a cause for celebration and ceremony because the baby is seen as a gift from God.

Look up Luke 2:21–4. The baby Jesus was first circumcised and then presented at the Temple according to Jewish ritual. People of all religions have special rites and ceremonies for the birth and naming of a child. Have you been to a Christian baptism? Discuss what takes place there and its meaning.

b) Make a summary in your notebooks of the case both for and against using 'artificial' methods of birth control.

c) Look carefully at the arguments both for and against abortion. Remember that there can be a middle way between believing it is always wrong or believing it is always right for the woman to choose. Write down the options in your notebook.

Arrange a debate on the subject after trying to discover further arguments both for and against it.

d) The contraceptive pill can have harmful side-effects. Discuss the view that it is better to take it than to have an unwanted pregnancy.

e) *'Both men and women are responsible for deciding whether or not to have a child.'* What do you think?

10 The Human Embryo: Infertility, Research

Children are the expected and normal outcome of marriage. Many people do not realise, however, that about one in ten couples are **infertile**. Couples, therefore, who want to have children of their own and for various reasons are unable to do so, can become deeply unhappy and frustrated. In the past, those who strongly desired children could either become **foster parents** or could **adopt** children. (To foster a child simply means to look after it for a period of time; to adopt a child means to become its legal guardian until it comes of age.) Today, however, there are fewer healthy babies available for adoption.

'We're so proud of our son!' This 'Dr Barnardo's boy', adopted as a teenager, is now a successful Army Officer trainee.

☐ Why do you think there are fewer babies available for adoption than in the past?

On the other hand, infertile couples may try to solve their problem by using new medical and scientific techniques.

Techniques for fertilisation

Artificial insemination (husband) (AIH)

This has been used successfully for several years by couples who cannot produce the semen and ovum through normal sexual intercourse. In these cases the male semen is planted in the woman's womb by 'artificial' methods.

Artificial insemination by donor (*AID*) has been used when the husband is infertile, or where there is a danger of passing on an inherited disease.

In vitro fertilisation (husband and wife) (IVF)

Fertilisation normally happens in the mother's fallopian tube. In vitro fertilisation is a technique for fertilising the ovum outside the mother's body, under laboratory conditions. (*In vitro* is a Latin term for 'in glass'.) In order to increase the chances of success, doctors usually transfer more than one fertilised embryo at a

31

Christine and Mickey Walsh, the footballer, with their test tube quads. The couple had been trying for a family for ten years before having fertility treatment.

time. They may also give the woman fertility drugs so that she produces more eggs. (Normally only one egg is produced each month.) After fertilisation, the embryo is returned to the woman's womb for a normal pregnancy.

Egg donation

If the wife is infertile, another woman may donate an ovum. This is then fertilised with the husband's semen and transferred to the wife's womb. The woman then bears a child who is not related to her.

Embryo donation

In this case, both the semen and the ovum are donated and fertilised in vitro. The embryo is then transferred to the womb. The child thus born has therefore four parents. Its physical parents donated the semen and ovum, while its social parents are the woman who carried the embryo in her womb and her husband.

Surrogacy or womb leasing

The surrogate mother agrees to bear a child for the wife who cannot become pregnant or for whom it would be dangerous. The husband of the childless woman usually provides the semen which is implanted in the surrogate mother by artificial insemination. Occasionally the people involved may agree the implantation through sexual intercourse.

The natural mother agrees to hand over the child at birth to the couple for whom she has carried the child. She may be paid quite a large sum of money for handing over the child in some countries, although in the UK this is now illegal. Under present law the couple have no legal rights in the matter and the surrogate mother has no legal claims on them.

> ☐ There have been several well-publicised cases of 'test tube' babies and surrogate mothers. Do you remember the names and details of the people involved? What did you think about them at the time? Before you come to any firm conclusions, however, read on.

Christian attitudes

The Roman Catholic Church does not agree with any of these techniques.

Protestants, however, are divided in their views, although all would agree that the status of human life and persons must be protected. They are deeply concerned that scientists should not step beyond certain clearly defined boundaries when they intervene in the course of nature.

Some Christians would object to AIH because it separates having children from sexual intercourse and because it breaks the exclusive union between husband and wife.

Many are also deeply disturbed by the 'test tube' baby technique as this goes a stage further in separating intercourse from new life. Instead of beginning life in the security of its mother's womb, the human being is fertilised in a laboratory. Egg donation and the still newer technique of embryo donation are yet further removed from normal procreation.

Christians also believe that paid surrogacy harms the dignity of motherhood. There is a real danger that the child is seen as a product to be bought for cash rather than as a gift of new life from God.

Strong ties of affection develop between a woman and the child she carries in her womb. They are 'bonded' together and the mother could find it extremely difficult to give the child up. In some cases she has refused to do so. It is also very tragic if shortage of money makes her go against her natural instincts.

We also need to consider the feelings of the child conceived by these scientific processes. At present we know nothing about what effects this may have upon a child's personal development.

> ☐ Discuss these points of view.

The Warnock Report

When Louise Brown was born in Oldham General Hospital in 1978 by in vitro fertilisation there was great public concern, as well as interest. In 1982 the government asked Dame Mary (now Lady) Warnock to lead an enquiry into Embryology and Fertilisation.

In July 1984 the report was published. It proposed that all treatment of infertility and research on embryos should be licensed. This would be the job of an independent body which would also set standards.

The report also recommended that donors of semen or eggs should only be paid their expenses. It further declared that it should be a criminal offence to commercialise surrogacy by setting up agencies or by any other method. All surrogate agreements should be recognised as illegal contracts which could not be enforced by law.

> ☐ Why do you think the Warnock Committee took such a strong line on these particular issues?

Louise Brown, Britain's first test tube baby, in July 1979.

Scientific research into human embryos

Research is possible because 'spare' embryos are produced when infertility is treated. As in vitro fertilisation and implantation often does not succeed, laboratories produce more embryos than they actually need. If an embryo is not implanted in the womb after four or five days it cannot survive as a human being. It can, however, be kept alive under laboratory conditions for several more days. Embryos have also been created for research purposes using the eggs donated by a woman who is being sterilised.

When the embryo is successfully implanted in the womb, by 14 days it begins to develop individually. By 20 to 21 days it forms cells for the brain, the spinal cord, the heart and so on.

The Warnock report recommends that after 14 days any spare embryo should be destroyed.

Christian attitudes

For those who believe that the human embryo becomes a human being at the moment of its conception, the whole idea of research without that person's knowledge or consent is quite wrong. It can further be argued that embryo research opens up all kinds of other abuses. It may lead to research on new-born babies, or retarded and mentally-handicapped people, even **genetic engineering**, i.e. changing the inherited pattern of a person so that you deliberately produce some qualities and get rid of others.

Those who see the human embryo as only a *potential* human being think that research is justified up to a limit of 14 days, provided there are very strict controls. This early research may extend our knowledge of inherited diseases such as Down's Syndrome and genetic disorders such as muscular dystrophy and cystic fibrosis.

There is much disagreement on embryo research. In 1984 an advisory body of the Church of England recommended support for licensed research on embryos up to 14 days old, but opposed the creation of embryos for research purposes. But in 1985, the Church of England General Synod supported the campaign to make all experiments on embryos illegal.

> ☐ If you were trying to measure human suffering, how high on the scale would you place infertility? Is it as bad as losing a child, for example, or not finding a husband/wife/partner with whom to share your life?

Over to you

a) The idea of surrogacy is not new. We find it more than once in the Old Testament. When Rachel could not produce the all-important heir for Jacob, she invited him to take Bilhah her personal slave, so that 'I may have children through her' (Genesis 30:3).

The same thing had happened earlier to Sarah, Abraham's wife, who offered her husband her slave, Hagar. Read the story in Genesis 16:1–6 and discuss the problems which arose because of this arrangement.

b) In a few known cases, the sister of an infertile woman has borne a child for her out of love. Discuss the difference between this kind of surrogacy and the paid kind.

c) Make notes in your book of the various techniques which can be used to solve the problem of childlessness.

d) Many childless couples have simply accepted this fact and have used their capacity for caring and responsibility by devoting their energies to children and adults in need.

Bearing this in mind, discuss the arguments both for and against the new methods described above.

e) After the Warnock report was issued, a woman's magazine surveyed some 3,000 of its readers. The survey came out strongly against experiments on human embryos and showed that ordinary people rather mistrusted scientists. They thought, however, that scientists would go ahead with research in any case.

Discuss the pros and cons of scientific research programmes.

11 Prejudice and Human Rights

Prejudice is an opinion which is formed before we know the facts of a situation. We are prejudiced if we look at others from a certain standpoint or slant, instead of seeing them clearly, honestly and justly. Prejudice has many causes ranging from simple ignorance to habit, fear, insecurity and intolerance. We shall see how these work out as we look at the four main categories of prejudice: sexual, social, racial and religious.

Hard physical work for an Indian woman in Ahmedabad while her husband sits in comfort. In 1980 a United Nations report showed that conditions for women around the world are getting worse, even though laws have been enacted to combat sexual prejudice.

Sexual

Our own particular culture has long been dominated by men. In other times and places (in early Mediterranean society for example) woman was ruler. The terms **patriarchy** (father) or **matriarchy** (mother) are used to describe these two kinds of society.

Throughout the developing areas of the world

Some churches in the UK and the rest of the world have had women pastors or priests for many years. Here, a female minister in Hong Kong greets her congregation. Would you have any objection to attending a church service presided over by a woman?

women are still under-privileged. They do very hard physical work to produce food and carry water, besides bearing and caring for their children. They have few opportunities for education.

> ☐ How many of these countries can you name?

It is only very recently that women in Britain and other Western countries have won equal rights. At the beginning of the century the **Suffragette movement** eventually gained for women the right to vote in elections (**equal suffrage**). In 1975 laws were passed giving women equal pay and equal opportunities. They now have equal rights in law relating to marriage and divorce. In spite of all this, there are far fewer women than men in many professions and in the top executive jobs in industry. And women cannot become Roman Catholic and Anglican priests. However, the 1985 General Synod of the Church of England agreed that women can become deacons and in the 1990s it will vote on women priests.

All this illustrates how ignorance and habit can produce prejudice. A woman has a different bodily function from a man because she actually bears and feeds the children. This makes her dependent and vulnerable during that time when she needs support. But there is absolutely no reason why she should be regarded as inferior to man, or as a second-class citizen. Social training and custom often make girls and women lack confidence about their skills in science and industry. Yet some of the world's greatest scientists have been women.

The United Nations Decade for Women (1976–85) stressed the need for equality, development and peace.

> ☐ Can you think of examples where boys and girls make sweeping judgments about one another? They may say: *'Girls are silly.' 'Boys are brutes.'*
>
> ☐ Look out for any news items which show prejudice against women.
>
> ☐ Should a young woman doctor be turned down for a job because she may marry and then have a child?

Social

Social prejudice springs from a false idea. It is assumed that being richer or better educated makes you superior to someone without these privileges.

In this country the Welfare State has brought many good social changes. It has provided health care and education for all and social security for the unemployed. Given equal opportunities, people from the poorest backgrounds have shown they can be extremely successful in all walks of life.

All is not as it should be, however. Recent figures suggest that nearly 11 million people are living on or below the semi-official poverty line, although about 23 per cent of government expenditure went on social services.

There are many quite different categories of very poor people ranging from the elderly and infirm to the young unemployed couple with several children.

> ☐ Discuss examples where social prejudice lumps these people together, saying, for example, *'They are only unemployed because they don't like work. They do not help themselves.'*

A few may be poor through their own fault. Millions of others are trapped by appalling conditions such as overcrowding, bad housing and ill health, with no prospect of anything better. Even if a job is found, the earnings could be less or no more than unemployment benefit. This situation brings great suffering and loss of confidence. It is sometimes called **the poverty trap**. People are caught in a trap because their poverty makes them unable to choose what they can do with their lives and their powerlessness helps to keep them poor.

Poverty in the United Kingdom. Comment on the contrasts this picture implies.

Unfortunately, where the majority are reasonably well off and only the minority are deprived (even though that minority may be nearly one in seven of the population) it is difficult to persuade people that change is needed. People are also slow to take action if they are prejudiced against the less privileged.

Jesus' teaching

Unfortunately most Christians have been just as prejudiced as anyone else in believing that the woman was inferior to the man and that wealth and rank made some men far more important than others. The teaching of Jesus, however, shows clearly that he was far ahead of his time in his attitude towards women. It is equally evident that he loved and reached out to the poor, deprived and socially outcast (see below for examples). In trying to understand his teaching, many individual Christians have led movements to change the position of women and to bring about great social change.

Over to you

a) Read (and, if you like, role play) Luke 7:36–50. The Pharisee is extremely critical that Jesus allows a social outcast such as a prostitute to touch him. Jesus cannot be a holy man to do so. The woman must have heard Jesus preach and offer forgiveness, so she comes and showers him with her love. Jesus receives her great love and publicly accepts her by forgiving her.

b) On another occasion (John 4:1–30) Jesus breaks all the religious, racial and social taboos (a *taboo* is something totally banned or forbidden). The woman in this story is a Samaritan (a half-caste in Jewish eyes). She is living with a man not her husband and as a woman she is regarded as an inferior being.

Think of modern examples of these stories.

c) Write out Paul's comments in 1 Corinthians 12:12–13 and Galatians 3:28. Here is the basic truly Christian attitude. Sexual, social and racial divisions should not exist for those who follow the way of Jesus.

d) Look up James 2:1–4. Discuss what he is condemning.

e) Read Luke 10:38–42. We know from another story (John 11) that the two sisters, Martha and Mary, lived with their brother Lazarus in Bethany. We can see here how Martha is worrying about having a good meal for Jesus and is annoyed that Mary does not help her. Jesus, however, does not think a woman simply belongs in the kitchen. He encourages Mary to seek after the kingdom.

Discuss this story, remembering that Jesus' attitude would have greatly surprised his hearers.

In our day, women are not so restricted and more go out to paid employment than stay at home. What part should men play in sharing the responsibilities of the home with working wives?

f) Do a project on a person or group relevant to sexual or social prejudice, e.g. Mrs Pankhurst, the Suffragette; the work of the Equal Opportunities Commission; or the Child Poverty Action Group.

Racial

The idea of racial superiority is found amongst all nations. The Greeks divided people into two groups – Greeks and barbarians. The Jews did the same – Jews and Gentiles. The Japanese used to believe that they were the direct descendants of the gods and therefore superior to all other races. This inbuilt feeling can also be found amongst the Chinese and amongst the white-skinned peoples of North America and Western Europe.

In the 1930s the horrors and tragedy of racial pride were seen in the rise and tyranny of Nazism in Germany. Adolf Hitler came to power with the National Socialist party. He systematically persecuted and then murdered six million Jews because of their racial origins.

> ☐ How would you reply to comments such as these? *'Black people are inferior to white.' 'White people are arrogant and unjust in their attitude to blacks.'*

The South African government has for many years had a policy of **apartheid**. This means keeping different racial groups quite separate by law. Under the South African system, four and a half million whites (of European origin) hold all the power and most of the land in a country of 29 million people.

But the colour of people's skins does not make them truly different from each other. There is no scientific reason for believing that different racial groups are less or more able to develop emotionally and intellectually, though it may be harder or easier to develop because of your cultural background.

Britain is now a multiracial society. In 1976 the Race Relations Act made it illegal to treat one person less favourably than another on the grounds of colour, race, nationality or ethnic origin. The Commission for Racial Equality was set up by the Home Office to enforce this law and to promote racial equality and good relations.

One example of its work is the 1985 report on Britain's immigration rules. The Commission considered that the rules were racist and aimed to prevent immigration from non-white countries in the **New Commonwealth**. (The New Commonwealth refers to countries that joined the Commonwealth in the 1940s onwards.) The four-year study claimed that one in 140 visitors from the New Commonwealth countries were likely to be refused entry, compared with one in 4,100 from the **Old Commonwealth** countries (Canada, Australia and New Zealand).

One in five wives of non-white British men were refused entry and 40 per cent of children were also refused, often after delays of three or four years.

The Home Office replied that the report ignored the fact that there was far greater pressure to emigrate from New Commonwealth countries and that, therefore, there was bound to be a greater number of problems.

> ☐ What do you know about the plight of Asian families which have been split by immigration rules?
>
> ☐ In some countries it is normal for parents to choose their children's marriage partners (**arranged marriages**). Discuss how such different cultural traditions might make officials suspicious and might even lead to wrong decisions.

Although Archbishop Desmond Tutu has won the Nobel Peace Prize, as a black man he is not allowed to vote in his own country. The Archbishop is against violent protest, but has warned the white government that apartheid must be abolished without delay if a bloodbath is to be avoided.

According to the Home Office, the government's aim is that 'all people in Britain, regardless of race, should be able to live and work together in an atmosphere of mutual trust and tolerance'.

> ☐ How far do you think this ideal is being put into practice?
>
> ☐ Do you think you are less prejudiced than your parents or grandparents?
>
> ☐ What difficulties do two people from different cultural and racial backgrounds face if they wish to marry?

Religious

We take for granted **freedom of conscience** and **freedom to worship** (or not) as we think fit. But there have been periods of religious persecution and prejudice in this country under both Roman Catholic and Protestant rulers. For example, although there have been Jewish settlers in England for about 900 years, it was not until the last century that a Jew became a Member of Parliament. His name was Benjamin Disraeli and he later became Prime Minister.

Religious persecution and prejudice are based on the belief that one's own brand of religion is the only true faith. Other forms of belief are seen as a threat. Thus in Iran today we hear that peaceful Baha'is are being persecuted by Ayatollah Khomeini's followers because their ideas and actions are thought to be dangerous.

Terrorist activity in Northern Ireland has been strongly condemned by both Roman Catholic and Protestant religious leaders. Even so, civil war is often fought under the banner of religion not just in Northern Ireland but in Lebanon and elsewhere too.

- [ ] What items on religious persecution have you seen in the news? Discuss those you have heard about.

- [ ] How do Catholics and Protestants view each other in N. Ireland? How have the tensions in that country helped to increase prejudice and fear?

Jesus' teaching

Jesus and his followers were clearly committed to people as people regardless of race or faith. His own nation thought itself religiously, morally

Corrymeela breaks down religious prejudice in Northern Ireland by bringing Roman Catholics and Protestants to live, worship and form friendships in the same community.

and racially superior to others. Nevertheless, Jesus healed all who asked him for help, whatever their background.

> ☐ People are often fearful that a group with a different social background, religion or race may try to gain power or influence. Discuss how such fears may create prejudice.
>
> ☐ *'Live and let live.'* How far can this view be applied to differences of race and religion?

Human Rights

In 1948 the United Nations issued a Universal Declaration of Human Rights. These are two of the most famous extracts from its many sections:

> All human beings are born free and equal in dignity and rights. They are endowed with reason and conscience and should act towards one another in a spirit of brotherhood.
>
> Everybody has a right to life, liberty and security of person.

The declaration was later transformed into International Law by two covenants. Since 1976 about 45 nations, including the UK, have officially agreed to these covenants. This means that the conditions of the Declaration are legally binding on the nations concerned.

In addition, the Council of Europe has adopted the European Convention for the Protection of Human Rights and Fundamental Freedoms which guarantees basic rights. For example, the European Commission has already ruled that the United Kingdom's law on telephone tapping interferes unjustifiably with the individual's right to a private life.

> ☐ The fact that all these matters are so hotly discussed in Britain and elsewhere in Western Europe shows the measure of our freedom and liberty. What do you know about countries where human rights are not valued in the same way?

Over to you

a) Read and discuss Luke 7:1–10. In Jesus' day, devout Jews would not mix with Gentiles at all. They felt that contact with Gentiles made them ritually unclean. Yet Jesus not only shows compassion for all races but praises the Centurion for his great faith.

b) Look up Luke 5:27–32 where Jesus eats with ritually unacceptable people. Put this story into a modern setting.

c) Read Mark 9:38–40. During the disciples' mission (Mark 6:7–13) John had apparently heard a man casting out a devil in Jesus' name. John rebuked this man because he was not a follower of Jesus. But Jesus said that many do his work of love and compassion without necessarily being followers of his. They are still part of his company and the disciples should not be possessive about their own status. What does this story teach about religious tolerance?

d) Arrange a forum of speakers from different Christian denominations and if possible from Jewish, Muslim, Hindu and Buddhist believers. Ask them to discuss the reasons behind religious prejudice and the answers to this problem.

e) Find out about the Corrymeela Community in Northern Ireland or similar groups which aim to break down fear and prejudice.

f) Read again this chapter on prejudice and make notes about the *causes* of prejudice, giving some examples.

g) Find out how to contact the Community Relations Council in your area. Ask one of its members to come and talk to your group at school.

OR Do a project on Britain as a multiracial society. Find out how many different ethnic groups there are in your locality. How happy are they? Do they feel that they are integrated?

h) Jesus' fundamental teachings about love of God and love of neighbour (Mark 12:29–31) have led many Christians into non-violent protest movements against violations of human rights.

Two very famous modern fighters for justice by non-violent means are Dr Martin Luther King of the USA (who was assassinated in April 1968) and Bishop Desmond Tutu of South Africa, the 1984 Nobel Peace Prizewinner.

Do some research leading to a project into the work of one or both of these men.

i) Study the Universal Declaration of Human Rights (see Appendix) and discuss any of its articles which are particularly relevant to the UK.

12 Work

Having a job is important for several reasons. It brings you into contact with other people with whom you learn to work. It helps you to acquire skills and to find personal fulfilment. It gives you a sense of belonging to the community and having a part to play in being of use to others. It provides money not only for the essentials of life but also for entertainment, hobbies and the many other things which bring us pleasure and comfort. But some kinds of work can also be boring, frustrating and even soul-destroying, with no reward at all but the pay-packet.

> ☐ How important is job satisfaction to you? If you had a choice of a boring but well-paid job or an interesting but badly paid job, which would you choose?

Unemployment

In recent years unemployment has grown. In 1960 in Britain there were fewer than half a million people out of work. In the 1980s there are over three million. There are many complex reasons for this, for instance:

1 The population has been increasing. In 1982, for example, there were a million more people looking for jobs than in 1976. Also many more married women are now going out to work.

2 The economy has not been growing fast enough to provide the new jobs required. And there is international competition from such countries as West Germany and Japan who produce certain goods more attractively and efficiently.

> ☐ Discuss the different makes of car that you see in your neighbourhood. How many are British made? Also look at all kinds of electrical equipment, such as cassettes, radios, television etc.

3 We are living in a technological age. In many industries machines do the job which was once done by human labour. For example, in previous times many men would be employed making bricks by hand, but they can now be produced entirely by automatic equipment (**automation**) which works by itself with only perhaps two people supervising the whole process. This applies not only to industry but also to farming and all kinds of manual labour. If you had owned a stately home at the beginning of this century, you might have employed forty gardeners to look after the grounds. Nowadays, with hedge trimmers, lawn mowers and other mechanical aids, seven people would be able to keep the place tidy.

> ☐ Discuss other examples of labour-saving equipment in the home and increased mechanisation in industry.

The **micro-chip** is another invention which is quietly revolutionising our lives. This tiny computer works rather like the human brain, receiving, storing, processing and reissuing information. The more widely computers are used, the more some kinds of human work will disappear. On the other hand different sorts of occupations will appear because computers need human beings to set them up and operate them. Computers should be regarded as the servants of people not their masters.

Different life-style

Some experts say that the unemployment situation will not get better until present *attitudes* are changed. For example, everyone should have a shorter working week and a shorter period of active work in their lifetime, retiring perhaps at 50 or 55, rather than at the present age of 60 for women and 65 for men. This would probably mean accepting a different standard of living or even a different life-style.

> - [ ] In what ways do you think your town or city would be different if everyone had a job? It might mean that there were many more part-time employees: would this matter? How would full employment affect shops, pubs, places of entertainment?
>
> - [ ] Would you be willing to take a part-time job if that meant your friend could also get some part-time work?
>
> - [ ] Would you be willing to share your work with someone else even if you did not know him or her at all?
>
> - [ ] You probably know people who have left school and who don't have a job. How do they feel about it?

The consumer society

It is said that we are living in a **consumer society**. In other words, everything is geared towards making us buy more and more goods. The advertisements that we constantly see on television and elsewhere suggest that if we buy a particular item to eat, drink, wear or use in our daily lives, we shall become happy and content.

One of the problems of living in a consumer society is that we may become dissatisfied, envious and bitter if we can't afford to buy the things which are displayed for sale. If we accept what the advertisers tell us, we may end up with a false perspective on the purpose of life.

Some people say that our society concentrates too much on producing luxury goods and instead should focus on providing essential services, such as cleaning up and improving our cities, using all our waste land, and creating better facilities for schools, hospitals, recreation and so on.

Youngsters, working with International Voluntary Service, clean up a river.

> ☐ Do you think that a bar of chocolate, a new car or any other consumer goods can bring happiness? Or do you think that happiness and contentment really come from other causes? These may be a certain state of mind, or appreciation of the natural world, or our relationships with other people. Can real happiness come from material goods, however satisfying these might be in their own right?

Work or employment?

Many people believe that we must get away from the old-fashioned attitude that *work* is the same thing as *employment*. Being employed actually means that you receive payment for a job which you do for someone else. Yet people undertake many activities which are really hard work, but for which they are not paid wages. These may be home jobs, such as housework, cooking, sewing, gardening, car or motor cycle maintenance, decorating or joinery. Others may work at staying healthy, through keep fit, athletics or a sport. Some may work in the community by visiting the sick, disabled and elderly or by taking on other voluntary jobs with deprived, disadvantaged or special interest groups.

> ☐ *'All too often people value you according to your job or lack of one.'* Would you agree that it is wrong to do so?

■■■■■■■■■■■■■■■■■■■■■■■■■
Over to you

a) Read Matthew 20:1–16. In this story about some labourers in a vineyard, Jesus' main point is that God's love is universal. God does not treat people according to what they think they deserve, but loves all people equally.

In the light of our present economic problems, the story can also be looked at another way. The last workers taken on by the master were presumably unemployed through no fault of their own, like millions today. If so, discuss whether it was fair of the master to look after the needs of all, or unfair, as the first workers thought.

b) Massive unemployment may well be here to stay. One possibility is that everyone should have a living wage, whether employed or not. What do you think about this idea?

c) Jesus was unemployed. While his father Joseph was alive, Jesus worked for him as a carpenter, then later continued working to support his family (Mark 6:3). When he gave up his job he travelled about the countryside teaching and healing (Mark 6:31–4). He and his disciples were often made very tired by their strenuous work with people (Mark 4:38; 5:30–1).

Discuss the false impression which is created when the phrase 'out of work' is used to describe unemployment.

d) Read Proverbs 6:6–11. What is being criticised here?

■■■■■■■■■■■■■■■■■■■■■■■■■■■

13 Spare Time

To simplify matters we could say that there are two basic approaches to life. One is the *passive*. This means we let things happen to us; we are content to be entertained, to let others make our important decisions and to have most things provided for us. The other is the *active* approach. This means we learn enough about ourselves and the situation in which we live to make our own decisions. We try to create our own entertainment and to use our opportunities and gifts to the best of our ability. Probably most of us are a mixture of both passivity and activity, of laziness and energy. We all need times of rest and quiet as well as times of activity.

> ☐ Do you plan what you will do in your spare time or do you simply let things take their course?

A day of rest

Judaism, Christianity and Islam all believe that it is essential for human beings to keep a holy day once a week. This is embodied in the idea of the sacred day, which is also a day of rest for the Jew and Christian (Exodus 20:8–10):

> 'Remember the sabbath day, to keep it holy. Six days you shall labour, and do all your work; but the seventh day is a sabbath to the LORD your God; in it you shall not do any work.'

The first followers of Jesus were Jews, so they kept the Sabbath (Saturday), the last day of the week, as their holy day, but they had the amazing experience of the risen Christ on the first day of the week. Therefore Sunday became for them a special day of meeting and worship (Acts 20:7; Revelation 1:10) to celebrate the resurrection. So our own weekend developed.

For Islam, the sacred day is Friday, when all Muslim men should attend the midday session at the mosque.

> ☐ Do you regard Sunday as a holy day, a day set apart for special purposes, or is it just a day of leisure?
>
> ☐ Do you think shops, pubs and places of entertainment should be open just as freely on a Sunday as on any other day? Which section of the population might suffer most if restrictions were lifted?

Using our spare time

It is one thing to plan how to occupy your time when you are still at school and probably have homework to do. But it may be quite different when you have left school and are either in employment or 'out of work'. Then boredom can set in, either because the job is mechanical and repetitive or because there is no job at all.

If you live in an area where there is high unemployment, the ability to get a job may be something outside your control. You may have the right attitudes towards work but simply be unable to find it. Even if your spare time is forced upon you, however, you can choose what to do with it, and if you have learnt to use your spare time creatively whilst at school, this will help you later on.

As human beings we can and should make conscious decisions about what to do with our time. When we use our ability to choose, this helps us to develop as people. Then others cannot make use of us against our will. Here are some suggestions for leisure activities:

1 Develop hobbies which require certain skills. Some of the athletes who won medals in the Los Angeles Olympics (1984) were unemployed.

2 Make a habit of reading. Public libraries are full of thousands of books on every topic under the sun. You have a very wide choice of books on any one topic and this reading may also help you in any further training you undertake.

3 Begin to appreciate the natural world in which we live. Many young people have done exciting things to improve the environment. They have cultivated waste land in decaying urban areas to produce vegetables, helped to clean up canals and waterways, and so on.

4 Give help to someone or to a particular group of people in the community, for example the elderly or disabled. (See Resources section for details.)

5 Join some kind of fellowship or club so you can mix with other young people regularly.

6 Take time to be by yourself. Think through your ideas both about yourself and others.

> ☐ Discuss which of these suggestions appeal to you and write them down in order of preference.

Jesus' teaching

Jesus tells a striking story about the use and misuse of talents or abilities. In it he underlines his belief that if you don't use your gifts and opportunities you will lose them. Then the chance which has gone may never come back. (See 'Over to you'.)

Some of Paul's friends in Thessalonica had given up work because they expected the end of the world any day. Paul urged them strongly to stop leading a life of idleness (2 Thessalonians 3:10–11, 13):

> If any one will not work, let him not eat. For we hear that some of you are living in idleness, mere busybodies, not doing any work... Brethren, do not be weary in well-doing.

Over to you

a) Read Matthew 25:14–29. It seems that the master understands his servants and their abilities quite well. He gives each a different sum of money to look after. It is the man with the smallest responsibility who does nothing. Either he is too lazy to act or he is too afraid of making mistakes.

Discuss modern examples to show that people who fail to make the most of their talents and gifts may end up by making a mess of their lives.

b) Write down what you see as your own potential and gifts. What further training do you need so as to achieve your ambitions? Make a chart showing how you now use your spare time and see whether in fact you are drifting or being creative.

c) Paul worked hard to support himself (Acts 20:33–5) and he was very sharp with his friends in Thessalonica who gave up work thinking that the end of the world was due at any time.

In Paul's day much of the work was done by slaves, and free men were self-supporting rather than employed. A free man worked to support his family and people paid him for what he produced.

Discuss the differences between that kind of society and our own.

d) Do a project on unemployment in your area. Find out what percentage of people are involved and what is being done to help them make good use of their leisure; for example, are there any self-help groups?

14 Money

In the Western world, money is especially important. Its value lies in what it will buy: food, clothes, warmth, a place in which to live, a pension for one's old age. It can also provide the extras in life such as holidays, entertainment, music, art, books and other kinds of pleasure.

> ☐ Assume you have only a very limited income. What are the main essentials on which you would choose to spend your money? List them in order of importance, saying why.

We live in a society which makes it very easy to overspend. Advertisers try to persuade us that we must have their goods. They encourage us to think that possessions bring happiness. If we are short of cash, we are told we can buy what we want now and pay for it over a period of time. Of course this is usually the only way that people can buy their own homes, as property is very expensive. In such cases, individuals make an agreement with the bank or building society and pay back the loan over many years. Before we enter into any hire purchase agreement, however, we have to be sure of what we are doing. Do we *need* the new car or video? Is it a luxury? If it is a luxury, can we really afford the repayments? We should not make agreements that may leave us badly in debt, or make it hard to pay for essential food and heating.

> ☐ List some of the things which you would very much like to possess but know are luxuries you can live without. If you compare your list with other people's you will find how different people's tastes and ideas are.

The limitations of money

Money cannot buy love, friendship, peace of mind or contentment. It cannot give the satisfaction which comes from doing a job well. It cannot encourage you to make the most of your personality and talents in arts, crafts, sports or other skills. Lack of money can cause ill health or **malnutrition** (a shortage of essential foods), disease or death. But money itself cannot buy health (even though it may buy care during an illness). Therefore we need to see money in perspective. It is a useful and necessary means to obtain life's basic essentials.

The misuse of money

There is a rather cynical saying: 'Every man has his price.' This means that we can all be persuaded to act against our best principles. A large sum of money, for example, may corrupt people into acting dishonestly or disloyally. When people fall into this kind of trap it is because they have a false sense of the value of money. Peace of mind comes from self-respect, personal integrity or honesty and having the trust of others. It does not come from a fat cheque gained dishonourably.

> ☐ Can you think of examples where money has brought out the worst in someone?

Gambling

In Britain, gambling is legal and takes many

forms. Some are harmless, some not, depending largely on the gambler's attitude of mind. There can be very little wrong with spending a few pence each week on the football pools. But for some people gambling becomes an obsession. They risk large sums of money and their families suffer.

It is natural to want excitement and adventure in life. If existence seems rather dull, someone may stake money on a game of chance or a sporting event in the hope of adding a little spice to life. But if you take excessive, foolish and selfish risks with money, it can lead to tragedy.

Jesus' teaching

Jesus was very clear in his attitude towards money. He lived in a world which contained both extreme poverty and riches. He saw that a man's desire to obtain wealth would fight against his desire to serve God (Matthew 6:24):

> 'No one can serve two masters; for either he will hate the one and love the other, or he will be devoted to the one and despise the other.'

If someone loves wealth he grows selfish and indifferent to other people's needs (Luke 16:19–31). Money can also give a false sense of security. The rich man who intended to eat, drink and be merry on the proceeds of his wealth, died before he could do so (Luke 12:13–21).

Paul wrote (1 Timothy 6:10):

> The love of money is the root of all evils; it is through this craving that some have wandered away from the faith and pierced their hearts with many pangs.

Amusement arcades offer tempting ways of losing one's money. Are they totally harmless?

An exciting pools win. What problems can such wins bring to an individual or family?

He knew that the early Christian community survived because all the members generously shared what they had with each other.

Jesus contrasted earthly with heavenly treasure (Matthew 6:19–21). In all his teaching, Jesus emphasised that people need a proper perspective on life. What really matters is the individual's relationship with God and with other people, not his or her possessions.

☐ Do you know where your money goes?

☐ Do you discuss money with your family?

☐ Do you save up for things you want?

☐ When you plan or budget your money, do you consider what you might want to give away to others?

Over to you

a) Read Luke 16:19–31. It may well be that on this occasion Jesus was using a well-known tale. The story drives home his criticism of the rich man's utterly selfish behaviour to the poor man at his gate. We need not think that Jesus personally believed in 'everlasting torment'. The whole of his life shows that he wanted people to act generously because they were convinced it was right to do so, not out of fear.

Put this story into a twentieth-century setting, adding your own comment.

b) Read Matthew 6:1–4 and Mark 12:41–4. In the first passage Jesus criticises those who give away money simply to gain approval. In the second, he praises the woman who has given at great cost to herself.

Discuss other examples of both kinds of giving.

c) Read Mark 10:17–31 and Luke 19:1–10. Jesus always treated people according to their special needs. Although the first rich man was very good, he could not give up everything to become a disciple. The second man had been very dishonest, but he saw clearly what he must do to put matters right.

Think of and discuss modern comparisons with the two men. Remember that when the first man refused to become one of Jesus' disciples, he missed the chance to do something quite unique. Money was more important to him than this special opportunity.

d) Look up and discuss Luke 12:13–21 and Matthew 6:19–21. Talk about the meaning of the sentence: 'For where your treasure is, there will your heart be also.' Write down Matthew 6:24.

e) Work out a budget for the living costs of a family of four. How much of the income might go on hire purchase agreements and mortgage?

f) Try to find out the amount of money which is spent each year on various forms of gambling in this country.

15 Addiction

It is one thing to speak lightheartedly of someone being a football addict and quite another thing to recognise that a person is addicted to a dangerous drug. To be an enthusiastic or even fanatical football supporter cannot do you any harm, unless you get violent and aggressive about it. But drug addiction means that you are compelled by a strong inner impulse to take something, even against your own better judgement. This means that the drug itself has taken over control of your will, often with tragic results.

What is a drug?

A drug is a plant or chemical which alters the way the mind or body works. People have always looked for relief from different kinds of pain. These may be physical (headaches, for example), emotional (grief over the death of a loved one) or psychological (stress may prevent people from sleeping, for instance). In the past, pain has been relieved by medicines made from natural products such as herbs, fruit or flowers. Nowadays special chemical preparations are also used to make drugs.

There are many different types of drugs but, broadly speaking, we can divide them into several groups:

1 **Stimulants** (Amphetamines, Cocaine). These increase mental or physical activity. Users can feel more energetic, alert and confident, but some may feel anxious, restless and irritable.

2 **Sedatives** (Barbiturates). These depress the normal functioning of the brain. They can soothe, calm and help people to relax, but can also produce drowsiness and lack of interest.

3 **Tranquillisers** (Benzodiazepines, such as Valium, Librium and Ativan). These relax the muscles and reduce anxiety. They can also lead to drowsiness and forgetfulness.

4 **Hypnosedatives** (Sleeping pills). These are used medically to calm people down and help them to sleep.

5 **Narcotics** (Opium, Morphine, Heroin). These act on the nervous system and can produce a feeling of well-being and contentment. They are used to relieve physical pain, but some users experience nausea and vomiting.

6 **Hallucinogens** or 'mind benders' (LSD, Mescalin). These completely change a person's state of mental awareness, causing delusions and fantasies.

7 **Cannabis, Marijuana** (known as pot or hash). This has a complex action on the brain being an hallucinogen and also a sedative, so that the users can feel both relaxed and confident, believing that they see things 'as they really are'.

8 **Delirants, Solvents** (Glue, fuel vapour etc.). Sniffing these fumes causes effects similar to drunkenness.

Doctors use some of these drugs to treat a wide range of illness. Chemists can sell some mild non-addictive drugs such as 'pain-killers' without a doctor's prescription, but the buyer must still follow the directions on the bottle

AT FIRST HE WAS SURE HE'D NEVER BECOME A HEROIN ADDICT.

NOW HE'S NOT SURE HE'LL EVER BE ANYTHING ELSE.

Take heroin and before long you'll start looking ill, losing weight and feeling like death. So, if you're offered heroin, you know what to say. **HEROIN SCREWS YOU UP**

carefully. Abuse or misuse arises when people take drugs without medical supervision or take more than the stated dose.

☐ Discuss differences between using a drug medically and drug addiction.

The legal position

☐ Consider the difference between those who peddle drugs for profit and those who take them because they are addicts. In your discussion look into the meanings of the words 'exploiter' and 'exploited'.

The 1971 Misuse of Drugs Act makes various kinds of drugs illegal and lists them in order of danger. You may not supply or possess any listed drug without medical supervision.

The Act punishes the illegal supplier of drugs far more harshly than the person who receives or possesses them.

Alcohol and tobacco

Many experts classify all alcohol and tobacco as drugs. Some however would argue that the valuable minerals in some alcoholic drinks give them good food value.

It is perfectly legal to buy alcohol and tobacco if you have reached the legal age. It is, of course, illegal to be drunk and disorderly, as this causes a public nuisance. There are great differences between the moderate or social drinker and the excessive drinker, the person who drinks him or herself unconscious and the alcoholic (the addictive drinker).

Alcohol is a *depressant*. Nicotine (tobacco) is a *stimulant*.

Causes of addiction

The reasons why people become dependent on drugs are very complex. Here are a few examples:

1 Someone may start to smoke because she/he is nervous and lonely. Gradually the occasional cigarette grows into the compulsive habit of 30–40 a day.

2 Someone else starts to drink because she/he is bored, frustrated and craves some outlet from routine. Gradually the single glass of beer taken in a pub is not enough and the person consumes many pints daily.

3 Young people may be tempted to experiment with smoking cannabis or inhaling heroin because they are dared to try something new, perhaps by an older person. Cannabis may lead people to try more dangerous drugs, and when they try heroin they find they are 'hooked' even after only a few experiences and simply cannot give it up.

In 1986, 1 in 4 schoolchildren in Greater London had sniffed solvents, yet it can cause brain damage and death.

4 A young boy or girl who cannot buy alcohol may imagine it would be interesting to be drunk or may wish for excitement. Such children may be misguidedly encouraged to sniff some **solvent** which contains chemicals and may find themselves addicted. In some cases this dangerous habit has caused death by suffocation. Seventy-one young people died from solvent abuse in 1984.

> ☐ Can drugs ever truly 'solve' problems? Remember that the improvement in mood is only short-lived. When the change wears off, people may find that they need more and more of the drug if they are to forget their problems. This is how dependence sets in.

Consequences of addiction

The dangers of tobacco are now widely known. For example it has been linked with cancer of the mouth, throat and lungs and with heart disease. That is why all tobacco advertising carries a Ministry of Health warning of the dangers. Too much alcohol can permanently damage the stomach, the brain, the liver. Addiction to either tobacco or alcohol can lead to death. Every day in the UK between 150 and 280 people die early as a result of their smoking and drinking habits.

Many social problems arise from excessive drinking, such as accidents on the road and at work, crimes of violence and broken family relationships.

No drug is completely free from side-effects. That is why the more powerful ones must be taken only under medical supervision. Drugs such as heroin and LSD (Lysergic Acid Diethylamide) are particularly addictive and dangerous in their effects. Heroin poisons the liver and kidneys; it can cause tuberculosis and it frequently leads to an early death. LSD produces serious mental disorders which in some cases are incurable. Solvents produce various skin complaints, sleeplessness and depression.

Drug dependence sets in when the body cannot work without a regular dose of the drug. If this is not available the victim feels serious withdrawal symptoms, such as violent muscular cramp, sickness, diarrhoea and mental distress. Misuse of drugs also causes changes of personality. Addicts lose interest in their job, friends and family and they show symptoms of mental confusion.

Treatment

1 Prevention is better than cure. Therefore it is very helpful for people to learn all about what addictive drugs are made of and why they are dangerous. For example, the campaign on the health risks of tobacco smoking has been very effective. Far fewer people in the UK smoke now than even 10 years ago.

2 It is good to stop and think before it is too late. When personal problems arise, try to look for different and safe answers, instead of escaping. Those in difficulty may talk over their crisis with a friend or counsellor (such as the Samaritans provide) or may seek proper medical advice.

3 If dependence sets in, then medical treatment is available. Now that there is greater research into addiction, the prospects of recovery are more hopeful.

4 Rehabilitation. Those who have been rescued from addiction need great support and help to enable them to return to normal life.

Tobacco firms (or breweries) try to link themselves with good health by sponsoring sport. Should they be banned from doing so?

☐ The drink and tobacco industries spend massive amounts of money on advertising. Discuss whether this could persuade people into excess or addiction.

Christian attitudes

Christians reject the misuse of drugs which distort and destroy the human personality.

Some Christians think the only way to solve the problems of alcoholism is by total abstention (not drinking at all under any circumstances). Others believe that occasional and moderate drinking is a pleasant and harmless way of relaxing and enjoying the company of one's friends.

All Christians agree, however, that too much alcohol can lead to tragic consequences. They therefore try to be self-disciplined and self-controlled whether or not they are total abstainers, smokers or non-smokers.

Discuss the various categories of drinkers and the arguments both for and against being a non-drinker.

Over to you

a) Read Romans 14:3–4, 13–18. Paul is writing to a multiracial community of Christians who have had serious disagreements over food. He urges them to tolerate and to love one another, not judging each other but trying to understand each other's problems.

How could Paul's advice help a family or other people who were trying to support someone with a drink problem?

b) When people get drunk, are they having a good time – or a bad time?

c) Ask someone from Alcoholics Anonymous to come and talk about the valuable work this voluntary society is doing among alcoholics.

d) Read 1 Corinthians 15:33–4; 1 Timothy 5:23; Ephesians 5:18. Discuss the various pieces of advice given in these letters.

e) What did the poet John Donne mean when he wrote, 'No man is an island'?

How does it link with Paul's view that his body was not his own and he could not simply do what he liked with it (see 1 Corinthians 6:18–20)?

Discuss both these ideas in connection with smoking, alcohol and drugs.

f) Do a project on one of the ways in which people are trying to help rehabilitate those who have become addicts.

16 Violence

We are all capable of violent behaviour but fortunately very few of us lack self-control and use actual violence against others. It is said that we are living in a violent society but probably all communities have had their violent aspect. Violence creates more violence. It is a vicious circle.

Children

It is a sad fact that some parents neglect or even ill-treat their children. Thousands of boys and girls today are in need of the basic care and protection which the law requires.

> ☐ Discuss the circumstances which might make a parent behave cruelly: he or she might be ill in body or mind, or so poor that he or she ceases to care. A woman might be beaten by her husband or partner.

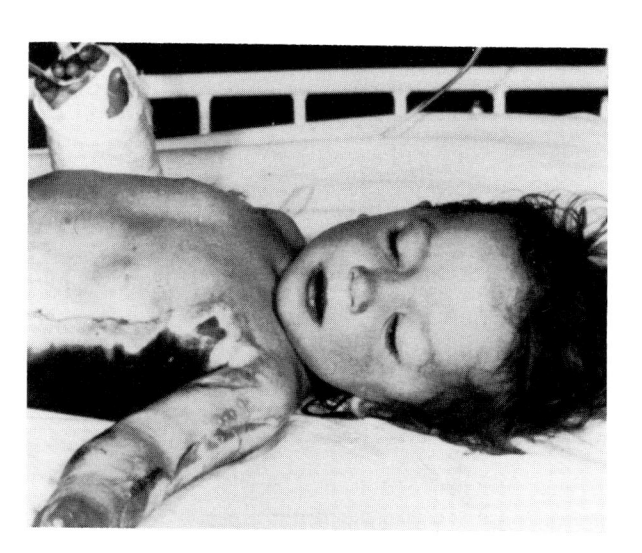

If parents don't care about their children, are not interested in them and beat them when they are troublesome, the end-product may be the boy or girl who is a bully at school. And unless the bully at school learns to understand himself and to change his feelings and pattern of behaviour, he eventually becomes the parent who in turn ill-treats his children.

According to the findings of a Scandinavian professor, one child in twenty is a bully and one child in twenty is a victim in Scandinavian schools. This professor started his research into violence in schools as a result of the tragic suicides of three children aged between 10 and 12 in the northern part of Norway. Each had been bullied at school.

> ☐ Do you know a bully in your school? Do you know a victim? If you have a bully, what do the rest of the class do about it; and the victim? How can we help each other in this respect?

The community

Successful bullies think well of themselves and believe that violence solves conflicts and helps them get what they want out of life. They do not think or care about what happens to those on the receiving end, or may even regard their victims as worthless.

We have laws to prevent or to punish violent action such as murder, manslaughter (killing a person without meaning to), wounding, robbery and burglary. But many personal acts of violence are never reported to the police by the victims. And the criminals responsible for reported violence are not always found out.

> ☐ Look at a recent newspaper and discuss any aspect of violence in the community which is reported there.

The media

Many believe that one reason for increasing violence in society today is the harmful influence of television programmes and videotapes. A report sponsored by MPs, peers and leading churchmen suggested that more than 40 per cent of seven- to 16-year-olds have at some time seen a video 'nasty' and the same percentage have a video recorder in their homes.

> ☐ How much control do you think your parents should have over what you watch on television or at the cinema or on video?

Under the 1959 Obscene Publications Act certain very violent films have been successfully prosecuted, which means they may not be shown in public. Even so, many of these films are now available on video. Some MPs are trying to change the law, so that the sale and hire of such videos can be stopped.

We need much more research into the effects of screen violence on viewers, especially children and teenagers. Already some evidence from the USA suggests that children become more aggressive when they see violence frequently on the screen.

> ☐ From your own experience would you agree with this research? How much do you think you are influenced by violent programmes? Do they cause nightmares? How much do we imitate the behaviour we see on the screen?

Vandalism

The Vandals were Germanic peoples who went on the rampage through much of Europe and North Africa in the fourth and fifth centuries, destroying many beautiful and precious books and works of art. They have given their name to the modern vandal: any person who wilfully or spitefully destroys and damages public or private property or the beauties of nature. A typical example of vandalism is when a public telephone box has its windows smashed and the telephone wrecked so that it is unusable. This does no good to the destroyer and causes great hardship and inconvenience to the local community who use the telephone.

It has been suggested that some young people feel so disillusioned with the society they live in that they wreck something belonging to it as a form of social protest.

However, vandalism does not cure anything. At its worst it causes tragedy or sorrow; even very minor vandalism is a great waste of public effort and finance which could be better spent. For example, the money needed to repair damage could have been used to create sports facilities and leisure centres.

> ☐ Discuss examples of vandalism that you may know about, and possible causes.

Rambo's Spitting Image *puppet. Why is this type of violence so popular?*

As in school, so in the community, the violent individual chooses as victim someone who is physically weaker than him or herself. Thousands of children are badly treated by their parents every year. Every week a child dies from injuries inflicted by its own parents. Hundreds of women are battered by the men they live with. Many old, vulnerable people are robbed and assaulted for money.

Of course the community as a whole is protected by the law. Our system of criminal justice aims to protect the community from disorder and anti-social behaviour (see the chapter on 'Law and Punishment'). One of the problems, however, is how far punishments such as fines or imprisonment deal with the root causes of violence.

☐ Can research tell us more about why some people take to violence? If so, what kind of research would you undertake?

☐ Is enough being done to help the victims of violence?

Millions of animals are used in experiments every year. Are all these experiments necessary? Should some be stopped?

Christian attitudes

Christians will try to understand and come to terms with themselves if they feel anger, bitterness or resentment which could flare up into violent action. By being honest with themselves, by praying deeply for help from God, by talking about how they feel with others who share their ideals, they learn to deal with the seeds of violence within.

Whatever the situation, we must try to see others as people who can be hurt just like ourselves. We will then learn to treat them with the respect and consideration we also need.

Over to you

a) Read Matthew 5:38–48. There are four ways of dealing with people who injure you. First you can pay them back with more than they gave you. Second you can give them exactly the same treatment as they gave you. Third you can detach yourself completely from the violence. Fourth you can forgive them, returning good for evil. But this does not mean that the bully or the criminal should escape punishment. Their actions must be stopped and they must if possible be helped to change their ways.

Jesus' words about a blow on the face, or the theft of clothing, must not be taken literally. Good can overcome evil. We must help to limit the violence, not spread it. In the second passage he is saying that we should see everyone, friends or enemies, as deserving care and understanding. This will give us the strength to forgive them if they hurt us.

Discuss these ideas. Do you think they only apply to us as individuals? Can they work for communities too?

b) Write down in your books these four ways of dealing with injury. Do they contradict one another?

c) Many people feel the need to protest against violent and cruel behaviour to animals. They argue that animals are particularly at risk because they cannot speak up for themselves.

Do some research into one of the many societies involved in this work such as the RSPCA, the Anti-Vivisection Society, FRAME, or Beauty Without Cruelty (See Resources section).

d) Write a project on vandalism in your local area. Find out from the local authority how much money ratepayers spend on repairing such damage each year.

17 Law and Punishment

A famous Greek philosopher, Plato, thought of justice as a state of balance or harmony. In a just world, all sections of the community would work well together, giving their individual talents happily, for the sake of everyone's good. An individual could also become a balanced person. This would mean that mind, feelings and physical energy worked in harmony together to make a whole personality.

We perhaps think of justice as fairness, or right treatment according to what we reasonably deserve. For example, if a woman steals some clothing from a shop and is caught in the act, she can expect to be punished. But if the woman is wrongly accused of stealing and is innocent of the crime, we expect her – in the name of justice – to be **acquitted** (declared not guilty).

> ☐ Discuss examples you know where justice has been seen to be done in school and in the home as well as in society.

1 The legal system in England and Wales is divided into Criminal Law and Civil Law. They have different courts. **Civil Law** deals with individuals who have committed civil offences against other individuals; for example, trespass.

2 **Criminal Law** deals with offences against the common well-being of the community; for example, possessing fire-arms without a licence, murder, theft.

3 Laws are passed by freely elected members of Parliament. A proposal for a new law is called a **bill**. When the bill has been passed by the House of Commons and the House of Lords it is given the 'royal assent' and is known as an **Act of Parliament**.

4 Courts are set up to deal with law-breakers and those suspected or accused of breaking the law. The Court decides the guilt or innocence of the offender.

5 The law presumes that a person is innocent until proved guilty. It is up to the **prosecution**, therefore, to make out a reasonable case. The accused person has the right to employ **defence lawyers** to put forward his/her case whether pleading guilty or not guilty. A person who cannot afford to pay legal fees is granted **Legal Aid** so that he/she may receive fair treatment.

Habeas Corpus

This Latin phrase means 'you must have the body'. In English law it stands for the fact that every accused person ('the body') has the right to be legally examined before a judge or a court. The authorities cannot detain you without proving that they have a reasonable case against you.

> ☐ Why is this right so very important? What could happen to the accused if it did not exist?
>
> ☐ Why is it also important that in the UK a person is presumed innocent until proved guilty?
>
> ☐ Do you know of any countries where these two laws do not operate? Find out more about such countries and about how their legal systems differ from ours.

Criminal Courts

Magistrates' Court

This deals with about 98 per cent of all cases, including all minor offences. It is presided over by at least three **Justices of the Peace**. These are lay people who are advised on points of the law by a legally trained justices' clerk.

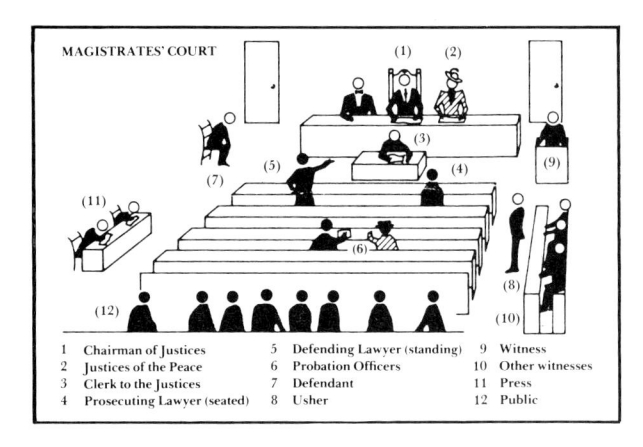

MAGISTRATES' COURT
1 Chairman of Justices
2 Justices of the Peace
3 Clerk to the Justices
4 Prosecuting Lawyer (seated)
5 Defending Lawyer (standing)
6 Probation Officers
7 Defendant
8 Usher
9 Witness
10 Other witnesses
11 Press
12 Public

Crown Court

This is presided over by a **High Court Judge**, a full-time **Circuit Judge**, or a part-time **Recorder**. At this court there is a jury which consists of 12 ordinary men and women who are on the electoral register (i.e. entitled to vote at elections). All the most serious crimes must come before a Crown Court, where the jury decides the guilt or innocence of people accused.

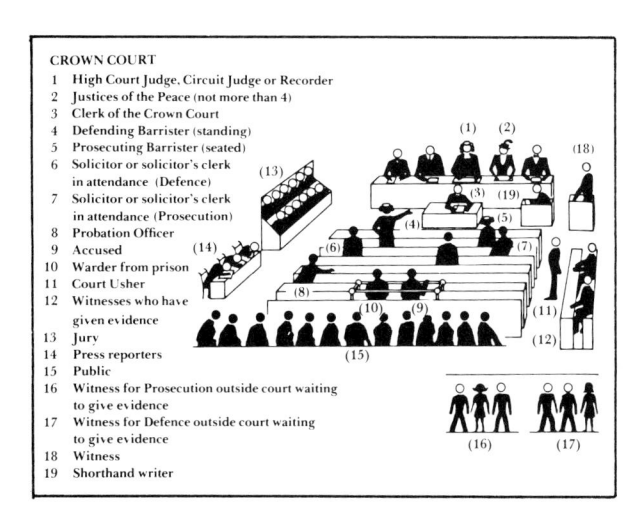

CROWN COURT
1 High Court Judge, Circuit Judge or Recorder
2 Justices of the Peace (not more than 4)
3 Clerk of the Crown Court
4 Defending Barrister (standing)
5 Prosecuting Barrister (seated)
6 Solicitor or solicitor's clerk in attendance (Defence)
7 Solicitor or solicitor's clerk in attendance (Prosecution)
8 Probation Officer
9 Accused
10 Warder from prison
11 Court Usher
12 Witnesses who have given evidence
13 Jury
14 Press reporters
15 Public
16 Witness for Prosecution outside court waiting to give evidence
17 Witness for Defence outside court waiting to give evidence
18 Witness
19 Shorthand writer

Juvenile Court

This is a special type of Magistrates' Court. It is presided over by two or three magistrates. It deals with young people between the ages of 10 and 17 and is held in private.

Coroner's Court

The Coroner holds an inquest into violent, sudden or unnatural deaths where the cause of death is not known.

The Police

It is the task of the police to prevent crime and enforce the law. Their powers are strictly limited and they do not normally carry firearms. As the force is relatively small, it is really the job of ordinary citizens to maintain law and order.

Punishment

If a person is found guilty then he/she is dealt with according to clearly defined principles and punishments. For example, someone convicted of a minor motor offence is usually fined a sum of money or has his/her licence taken away for a certain period of time.

A young offender may be sent to an **attendance centre**, a **detention centre**, a **community home**, a **youth custody centre** or put under the supervision of a **probation officer** or **social worker**, or ordered to take **Intermediate Treatment.**

An adult may be put on probation and may have to do **community service**, or may be sent to one of the several categories of prison available for different types of offender.

☐ Do some research into the places that a young offender can be sent to, and what it means if someone is put on probation.

☐ What does an offender have to do if given a Community Service order?

Intermediate Treatment (attending a special centre) allows young offenders to work for examinations while living at home.

Aims of punishment

1 *Retribution*: receiving what you deserve for doing wrong.

2 *Deterrence*: discouraging the wrongdoer from repeating his/her crime and others from following his/her bad example.

3 *Reformation*: making the wrongdoer into a better and more law-abiding member of the community.

4 *Protection of society* from the harmful behaviour of lawbreakers.

> ☐ Discuss examples of each of these four aims. Can all four aims be carried out together or are they contradictory?
>
> ☐ Compare these aims with the four ways of dealing with a person who injures you (see p. 56).

Release from prison

Many ex-prisoners are homeless and unemployed. After-care services aim to help prisoners resume a normal life when they come out of prison. Many voluntary organisations, some of which have a Christian foundation, take a special interest and care in the rehabilitation of former prisoners.

> ☐ Do you think that more severe sentences are the answer to the rising rate of crime?
>
> ☐ Do you think that going to prison can reform a criminal?
>
> ☐ What responsibility should society take to help the criminal change his/her ways?

Jesus' teaching

Look up Matthew 5:7, 38–42 and Mark 11:25. 'An eye for an eye' is a poetic way of talking about strict justice, such as **capital punishment** which demands that the convicted murderer should lose his/her own life as punishment.

Jesus tells us to look at things differently and he gives three examples, but we must not take them literally. Early Jews had only two garments, so to give away the second would leave a man naked. Jesus is talking about the spirit of active love which overcomes evil.

Civil liberties

A great deal of concern today is focused on people's civil rights and liberties. There is particular anxiety that minority groups might be discriminated against because of their colour, sex, political opinions or social status.

There has been much debate, for example, about whether the 1986 Police and Criminal Evidence Act has achieved a right balance between police needs and citizens' rights. Many

By contrast, since 1980 the police in Scotland must release a suspect after six hours of questioning unless a charge is made.

Pressure groups, such as the National Council for Civil Liberties, campaign on a wide range of issues where the law may intrude into the individual's liberty and responsibility. There is conflict between those who believe that the state is being given too much power to control people's lives and those who think these measures are necessary for national security and stability. One example is the fact that in 1984 everyone who worked at the Government Communications HQ at Cheltenham lost the right to belong to a trade union.

☐ Discuss how you yourself might react to long hours of questioning, even if you had nothing to hide and were quite innocent. Would it make any difference if you were of a different age, race, or sex, or less well educated, or hungry?

Over to you

a) Read Amos 5:10–15, 21–4 and 8:4–6. What kinds of injustice was the prophet protesting against? Do similar things go on today?

b) Read 1 Kings 21:1–19. Ahab was the king of the Northern kingdom of Israel. He had married a princess from Sidonia, Jezebel, who had brought her own religion with her to Israel. She believed that a king had the absolute right to do what he wanted with his subjects. When Naboth refused to sell his vineyard to the king, she arranged for him to be tried on a false charge of treason so that the vineyard eventually became the king's property. Although his life was in danger from Jezebel, the prophet Elijah visited Ahab to tell him of God's anger at this deed.

Put this story into a modern setting and think of other examples where people use power and money very unfairly so as to get what they want.

c) Do a written project on the work of NACRO (National Association for the Care and Resettlement of Offenders),

OR on the life of the social reformer Elizabeth Fry.

☐ What should relations between the general public and the police be like?

are worried that the police have the power to stop and search people in the street and hold them in custody for 96 hours without charge, even though this would be done through the approval of a special/extra Magistrates' Court.

The Law Society and the law reform group, Justice, pointed out that detention for questioning eroded and even destroyed the right to remain silent when questioned by the police. Only the most hardened criminals could hold out against persistent police questioning; the less experienced might give in to pressure and might possibly make a false confession.

18 Authority and Opposition

Parents

Authority is the power or right to give orders and make others obey. Our first experience of authority comes in the home where we learn to obey our parents. They tell us what we may or may not do when we are young, for our own good: 'Do not cross that busy main road on your own'; 'Do not speak to strangers.' Parents will also keep medicines away from young children and see that they are not in danger of burning or scalding themselves.

☐ Think of other examples where parents exercise necessary authority.

An inadequate parent might misuse power and authority to bully or ill-treat the child, but this does not mean that right parental control should be got rid of.

Teachers

At school there must be some order and discipline so that pupils can learn. Teachers' training and education have given them useful knowledge and expertise. It is in the students' own interests to acquire this skill and information. Usually the teacher has some kind of power to punish a difficult or disruptive pupil so that he/she can not prevent others from learning.

To do their jobs properly, teachers must have some kind of authority, even if a poor or inadequate teacher uses his/her power in an unfair way.

☐ Discuss how authority works in your school. Would it be better if there were no rules at all? What rules do you think are essential, if any?

Employers and trade unions

In any work situation certain rules must exist if anything is to be produced. An employer needs to enforce regulations such as getting to work on time. But employers also need to consult their workers properly. In the past, employers had too much power. They could pay too small a wage and dismiss workers who complained. But the trade union movement brought about better working conditions and laws have now been passed regulating terms of employment. Wages are generally fixed by agreement between employer and union. Workers can sue their employer for unfair dismissal or can get their union to act for them.

But the power of management and trade unions can still be questioned. Some would say that the trade union **closed shop** in Fleet Street, for example, is acting against individual freedom. (A *closed shop* is an agreement that only members of a particular trade union will be employed.) On the other hand, the power of management to close a works because they consider it is not making enough profit, may make employees protest that they should have been consulted before they lost their jobs.

☐ What can you find out about workers' co-operatives where all decisions are shared?

61

> Discuss some of the difficulties which could arise when a great many people have a voice in what should be done. Remember the proverbs: *'Too many cooks spoil the broth'* and *'Many hands make light work.'*

The state

Although we have far greater freedom in the United Kingdom than in many other countries, the state still has considerable control over us. We need an organised community under a central government for normal life to go on. The state has to maintain law and order, and to make sure that essential services exist for all its citizens. It also has to see that local government looks after the general welfare of everyone in its area.

Socialists and Labour supporters believe that a great deal of state control is necessary to ensure fairness for all. For example, land, transport services, natural resources such as coal, gas, oil, should all be **nationalised**. On the other hand, Conservatives think there should be more privately owned companies because they believe these are more efficient and that competition produces better and cheaper goods.

> What do you know about the main political parties? Who is your local MP?
>
> Why is it important to be informed about these matters?

Living in a **democracy**, we freely elect representatives to parliament every five years. The political party which gains a majority of seats forms a government. In other words, the people of the country run it through their chosen representatives. This is a form of power sharing.

When a person, party or military group takes control of a country and kills or imprisons anyone who disagrees, this is an evil use of authority. In the 1930s Adolf Hitler brought Nazism to power in Germany and proved himself an appalling dictator. During his time, at least six million Jews were murdered in concentration camps. **Totalitarian government** will not allow any rival party or loyalty. It cruelly puts down any opposition and insists on total obedience to the state. Absolute power can completely corrupt the dictator and his followers.

> Discuss the dictators and oppressive regimes that have emerged during this century in different areas of the world.

Dietrich Bonhoeffer was a German pastor executed by Hitler for opposing his evil regime. Find out about him.

Opposition to authority

We can all feel rebellious if we think we have been unfairly treated. And in our society we expect to have the right of appeal. We also take for granted the right to freedom of genuine conscience. A **conscientious objector** is someone who refuses to do something because he/she believes it to be morally wrong.

During the Second World War, conscientious objectors who refused to fight because they thought war totally wrong (**pacifists**), were allowed to do some other job, or were sent to prison. They were not shot as traitors by a firing squad.

A **dissenter** is someone who makes a peaceful protest against what he/she considers to be unjust or mistaken government policy. In a democracy, this dissent plays a valuable part in changing ideas.

> ☐ In 1984 thousands of unemployed people marched to declare their belief that they had a right to work and that the government should alter its economic policies. Discuss any marches and peaceful rallies you may have seen on television or taken part in yourselves.

In many countries the citizen does not have this form of public protest. When Argentina was ruled by a military junta, thousands of dissenters (especially students) simply disappeared and were never seen again. The democratic government which followed looked into these tragic deaths.

> ☐ Can you think of other countries where dissidents have disappeared or are imprisoned?

A **terrorist** is someone who makes violent protest against authority by shooting, kidnapping, bombing, wounding. In effect, the terrorist declares war on a particular system or policy of government and treats all ordinary citizens as victims. Many hundreds or thousands of innocent people can be injured or killed through terrorist acts. In a country where there are peaceful, lawful ways of changing conditions, all humane people must condemn the use of terrorism. And no right-thinking person wants to be ruled by the gun or hand-grenade. A reign of terror or civil war results from such methods.

Dissent in Eastern Europe – although people can be imprisoned for political activities in Poland, this photograph shows Poles marching openly in 1985 in support of Solidarity – a workers' movement formed in 1980 which was later made illegal by the government.

THE SPHERE

With which is incorporated "THE GRAPHIC"

The Empire's Illustrated Weekly

GANDHI TERMINATES HIS FAST UNTO DEATH—THE MAHATMA BORNE TO HIS EVENING PRAYER MEETING AT NEW DELHI AFTER HE HAD RECEIVED PLEDGES FROM HINDU, MUSLIM, AND SIKH LEADERS IN DELHI THAT THEY WOULD STRIVE FOR COMMUNAL HARMONY : It was while Mr. Gandhi addressed the meeting that a bomb exploded on the wall, about 50 yards away. No one was injured and the Mahatma went on with his sermon exhorting national unity

Fifteen times in the past thirty-five years Mr. Gandhi has used fasting as a method of bringing home his views in a forcible manner, and never has he been more effective in his achievement than now. His latest fast has demonstrated to the full his amazing influence over his fellow-countrymen, for after five days of symbolic self-immolation the Mahatma received assurances from all communities that they would carry out the conditions laid down for restoring communal harmony, primarily in Delhi, but ultimately throughout India. Meanwhile, halfway across the world at Lake Success Mr. Gandhi's fast has also made its influence felt, and the delegates of India and Pakistan came together this week in direct talks in regard to the Kashmir dispute. Whatever the eventual outcome of the dispute, it is certain that by his action Mr. Gandhi has, for the moment, at any rate, prevented a war between the two new Dominions Pictures taken during the fast are reproduced on page 140 of this issue

☐ Discuss various acts of terrorism that have happened in the UK and the suffering they have caused.

If evil is in power and peaceful protest is not allowed, this creates a terrible dilemma. Some people may then feel that they have to use physical force. For example, the murderous regime of General Amin in Uganda led President Nyerere of Tanzania to invade and force Amin into exile. Eventually the Tanzanian troops withdrew to leave Uganda to resolve its own problems.

☐ What kind of authority do you accept? Compare and contrast the bossy leader or bully with the leader who gets general agreement through discussion and reasoned argument.

Mahatma Gandhi

One twentieth-century figure who has inspired peacemakers throughout the world is Mahatma Gandhi (see opposite). His policy of non-violent protest roused a nation.

☐ Discuss what you know about Gandhi. Where did he come from? What religious beliefs did he hold? What resulted from his work?

Jesus' teaching

Jesus stressed the importance of understanding our inner motives for doing things. He rejected the way of violence to further his own cause (John 18:11). He would not let his disciples fight for him when he was arrested (Luke 22:49–51). He believed that justice and peace (i.e. righteousness) should only be brought about by self-sacrifice, love and non-violent protest and that people must always use good methods when they fight for a good cause.

Over to you

a) In Old and New Testament times slavery was an accepted part of life and women and children were thought inferior to men. A man had absolute authority as head of the household and rulers had great power over their subjects.

Nevertheless everyone was subject to God's authority and his moral laws. So in 2 Samuel 11:2–12:25 the prophet Nathan sternly rebuked King David for his crime against God. David had arranged the death of his loyal soldier Uriah so that he could marry Uriah's wife, Bathsheba.

Discuss the idea that people in authority must always act responsibly towards those they govern.

b) Jesus' great natural authority came from his own personal quality and honesty, not from any powerful position that he held. Discuss its effect on people as shown by Mark 1:21–2; 11:15–18.

c) Read Mark 12:13–17. All Jews hated having to pay Roman tax and being under Roman control. Jesus' enemies hoped to trap him by this question. If he said no to the tax, they would denounce him as a rebel. If he said yes, he would be very unpopular with the people. Jesus replied that it is right to keep the law of the state, but people's highest duty is to God and his moral laws. Where these loyalties conflicted, early Christians put their service to God first despite persecution. Look up Acts 5:27–9. The disciples had been arrested for preaching in Jesus' name.

d) Paul believed that all authority belonged to God, but that a good ruler could act as God's deputy (Romans 13:1). A Christian should therefore try to be a reliable citizen and should obey the state, unless it made evil rules. In that case, God's law would come first. Do you agree with his views?

e) A new window in Salisbury Cathedral is dedicated to Prisoners of Conscience who have died for their beliefs. Some newspapers regularly report on prisoners whose only crime is their political or religious opinions. Find out about some of these individuals.

Do a project on the work of Amnesty International.

f) Make a note in your book of the difference between a dissenter and a terrorist.

g) Write down the reasons why parents, teachers, employers, trade unions and governments have the right to some kind of authority.

19 Service

It is through our friendships and our daily contacts with other people that we develop fully as human beings. Learning to take responsibility is part of this process. For example, when we can, we help in the home by washing up, making the beds, doing the shopping and getting a meal ready.

> ☐ Discuss what further responsibilities you might take on in the family and at school.

As we grow older we see beyond the immediate circle to the wider responsibilities of the community.

The needs of others

Although our country is very wealthy compared with many others, there are still countless numbers of people in need.

The old and infirm

Men and women receive the state retirement pension when they reach the age of 65 (men) and 60 (women). Thousands of these pensioners lead active lives and give great service to the community for as long as their health and age permit. But there are also many old people who are in poor health and who suffer from various disabilities.

The state helps in many ways by enabling the OAP to get free medicine, reduced transport costs and other similar facilities. There are also a number of voluntary organisations, such as Age Concern and Help the Aged, who work with old people in need. And there are many ways in which old people can be helped on a neighbourly basis. For example, some schools organise a voluntary visiting rota to old people who may live alone, or in homes for the elderly, or in sheltered housing (where someone is always on duty to give help if a resident needs it). Volunteer youngsters might tidy up the garden, do small errands or simply have a chat with someone who has not seen anyone else that day.

> ☐ Do you do anything like this in your school? Discuss ways in which people of your age can help the elderly, remembering that older people also have friendship to give to the young, so it is not merely a one-way relationship.

Mentally or physically disabled

The 1981 Year of the Disabled made people aware that there are many isolated people of all age groups. Much practical work is now being done to enable them to take their proper place as members of the community. It is possible to provide special ramps for wheelchairs at pavement kerbs and at entrances to places of entertainment. Parking places can be reserved for disabled car drivers.

There is now a special wheelchair marathon race in the summer and a disabled (paraplegics) people's olympics. There is still much more to be done, however, especially in changing attitudes towards those who are disabled.

It is said that in any community, one person in ten has some kind of handicap or disablement. Many disabled hate being put into a special category. They simply want to be treated as people in their own right.

> How well do the fit and the handicapped mix together? What more can be done to help each group to understand the other?

The poor

Some people in our society are destitute (lacking the necessities of life) and homeless.

According to Shelter (the National Campaign for the Homeless), the plight of homeless people in the 1980s is worse than in the previous decade. The number of new cases coming for help to their housing centres is increasing each year. This view is also shared by Church Action on Poverty (an organisation formed from many Christian denominations). They report that thousands of people are not able to meet the basic energy needs for warmth, lighting and cooking.

Anyone receiving Supplementary Benefit is said to be on the poverty line and in 1985 it was said there were five million people dependent on benefit. There are about 15 million people altogether (over a quarter of the population) who are on the margins of poverty and who do not have any resources to meet emergency or unexpected expenses.

> Discuss how constant anxiety about money can ruin people's health and relationships.
>
> Discuss what strains and tensions arise when a family has just enough money to live on but not enough for any emergency. What kind of emergencies could happen to any family of four?

Jesus' teaching

Jesus' friends did not understand the kind of community which he was working to create. One day, on a journey up to Jerusalem for the Passover festival, he discovered that they had been discussing amongst themselves who was the greatest. On another occasion during the same journey, James and John (his two closest friends) asked him for the chief places in his kingdom.

Jesus told them that in his eyes true greatness lay in serving others (Mark 9:35). He himself had come not to be served but to serve, even to give his life for others (Mark 10:42–5). He saw the Messiah as the Servant of God. We can see this from the account of his mental conflict or temptations (Luke 4:1–13; Matthew 4:1–11). He chose the way of sacrificial love. And according to John (13:2–17), at the last meal they had together, Jesus washed his friends' feet.

Stewardship

We all have different gifts. How we use them is a matter of personal choice and also opportunity and education. Jesus warned that if we do not use what we have, we may end up losing that potential and that gift (Mark 4:25). He believed that his followers should be a clear and striking example to others. They should show the world how to live life to the full by caring for each other and generously helping those in need. Look up Matthew 5:14–16. They should be light in the darkness.

> What modern-day picture would you use to illustrate Jesus' meaning?

Christian attitudes

The early Christian community shared everything they had (Acts 2:44–7). Paul worked hard at his trade to support others who were with him, even though he spent most of his time preaching and teaching (Acts 20:33–5).

Christians today follow Jesus' teaching about service to others through education, social and welfare work. They may give their free time to support various agencies such as Shelter and the Samaritans (the people who give help to those who are desperate and suicidal). A few individuals, like Mother Teresa of Calcutta, have dedicated their whole lives to the dying and destitute.

Individual service

When we see the great need and the terrible problems that exist even in our rich Western society, it is tempting to think that there is really nothing much we can do. But experience has shown that the few dedicated individuals can bring about great social change. This was the case when the slave trade was abolished through the work of William Wilberforce and when major prison reforms happened thanks to the efforts of Elizabeth Fry.

Experience also shows how hundreds and thousands of people can be greatly helped by many small acts of service. If we each contribute our special gifts and are generous in our stewardship of time, money and energy, we can achieve a very great deal. For example there are now many work camps through which young people can take on some particular form of community service in their holidays. They may clear derelict land or help children create a play area for themselves.

■■■■■■■■■■■■■■■■■■■■■■■■■■■■
Over to you

a) Read Matthew 25:31–46. This parable about the Last Judgement is the climax of Matthew's account of Jesus' teaching. All the nations of the earth are there and the basis for judgement is quite clear: how did each person react when he/she met someone else in need?

If people gave help to someone else, they gave service to Jesus himself. The pictures of hell and eternal punishment should not be taken literally. They symbolise the fact that we destroy ourselves if we lead a completely selfish and heartless way of life.

Write down the various kinds of need which Matthew describes. Compare them with those mentioned earlier in this chapter.

b) Read John 13:2–17. Role play the story, thinking particularly about what Peter and Judas Iscariot must have felt like. It was Judas who betrayed Jesus to the Jewish authorities by telling them where and when he could be arrested. It was Peter who swore to die for Jesus but who three times denied that he knew him.

Afterwards, discuss what Jesus meant by saying 'a servant is not greater than his master'. Who was the servant and who the master?

c) 'If you know these things, blessed are you if you do them.' How are these words likely to influence a Christian's way of life?

d) Look up Luke 3:11 and 1 John 3:17–18. John the Baptist was urging his audience to be generous in the extreme! Remember that most of those listening to him would be very poor by our standards. In the second extract, the writer links the practical love of others with the love of God.

Discuss both these passages, linking them with today's problems.

e) Get someone from either the local Council for Voluntary Service or Community Service Volunteers to come and talk to your group about opportunities for service.

f) Work on a project about a twentieth-century Christian who has done outstanding service for those in need, such as Mother Teresa of Calcutta, Leonard Cheshire or his wife Sue Ryder.

g) Look again at your own gifts and your potential; in your own mind decide how well you are stewarding what has been given to you.

h) Do a project on what happened in International Youth Year 1985.

i) Try to find out as much as you can about the work of Shelter and in what ways it can be supported.

j) Jesus said that greatness in the kingdom did not mean holding power but giving humble service to others (Mark 10:42–4). Apply this to the life of Bishop Trevor Huddleston who worked in South Africa. He has always been brave and unselfish in speaking against racial discrimination.

■■■■■■■■■■■■■■■■■■■■■■■■■■■■

20 War and Peace

Old Testament views

The prophets dreamt of a time when peace and justice would exist throughout the whole earth. This would only happen when people obeyed God's moral laws (Isaiah 2:3–4). They also believed that there was such a thing as a holy war when people were called upon to defend their land from invasion or oppression.

At one time they even thought of God as a Man of War (Exodus 15:3) who would lead them to victory over their enemies, helping them to settle in the land of Canaan.

The prophets thought God used foreign invasions and oppression to punish his people for being unfaithful to him. When the Northern and Southern kingdoms fell to the Assyrians (722 BC) and Babylonians (586 BC), they saw these terrible disasters as the punishment which faithless Israel and Judah deserved.

Jesus' teaching

Jesus, however, was quite clear that violence did not achieve anything good. When his disciples wanted to fight against his arrest in the garden of Gethsemane, he said (Matthew 26:52):

> 'Put your sword back into its place; for all who take the sword will perish by the sword.'

He saw peacemaking as a god-like quality (Matthew 5:9). To be a peacemaker does not mean giving way about matters of truth. It is a positive and loving effort to bring together opposing sides so that they may learn to understand each other. Then they may eventually find

---

Say NO to PEACE
if what they mean by 'peace'
is the quiet misery of hunger,
the frozen stillness of fear,
the silence of broken spirits,
the unborn hopes of the oppressed.

Tell them that PEACE
is the shouting of children at play,
the babble of tongues set free,
the thunder of dancing feet,
and a father's voice singing.

Peace, freedom and justice go together.

To make war is simply to use force either to settle an argument or to gain a point. We can therefore have the seeds of war (i.e. physical conflicts) in the classroom and at home as well as in Northern Ireland and Lebanon. Making peace or war is a matter for all of us to think about whatever age we might be.

- ☐ Discuss examples where force is used to win an argument or settle a dispute.

some common ground and so reach a better relationship.

> ☐ Discuss situations where two friends quarrel and a third person tries to bring them together again.

The Just War

Many Christians believe that in some circumstances it is right to fight in defence of one's family, country and ideals. Over the centuries they have drawn up rules for a Just War:

1 A Just War can only be undertaken by the state's accepted leaders.

2 It must be fought against a definite injustice.

3 War must be formally declared.

4 All other methods must be tried first.

5 There must be a good chance of winning the war without inflicting so much suffering that it outweighs the possible good to be gained.

6 Innocent people not involved in the conflict must be protected, e.g. the old, the sick, infirm, women and children.

7 Soldiers must be controlled so that they do not murder, plunder or rape.

8 Winners must only seek justice and must be merciful in victory.

But modern methods of warfare make it extremely unlikely, if not impossible, that these conditions can be fulfilled.

> ☐ Look at any armed conflict taking place today, such as the war between Iraq and Iran, or the troubles in Afghanistan, the Lebanon or Northern Ireland and discuss ways in which any of the eight points given above have not been kept.

Even in the past, when local wars were fought by small numbers of professional soldiers, the civilian population did suffer in various ways. Shortages of food and water, disease, loss of home and family could all follow large-scale battles. War arouses barbaric and cruel behaviour as well as courage and loyalty.

Christians who believe in a Just War realise that Jesus himself refused to fight for his cause by violent means. They argue that this was a personal matter of individual choice and could not apply on a world scale. Evil has to be controlled, otherwise it would overwhelm everyone. Nazism was clearly a terrible evil, for example, in causing the murder of six million Jews. Therefore the Second World War came close to the definition of a Just War. Even so, the loss of life was appalling. Nearly 17 million military died, while double that number of civilians perished – almost 34 and one third millions.

> ☐ Discuss how these civilians came to die. What reasons were given for bombing large centres of population?

Pacifism

A minority of Christians of all denominations has always believed that war is morally wrong on every count. Such people have refused to take part in any armed conflict, sometimes at the cost of their lives.

Those who totally oppose war and believe that all disputes should be settled by peaceful means, are called **pacifists**. The term **conscientious objector** applies to those who for reasons of genuine conscience refuse to be conscripted into the armed forces, either in peace or war time.

The Society of Friends, often called Quakers, is one Christian group which has rejected war ever since the Society was founded over 300 years ago. Many have gone to prison for their beliefs, while others have risked their lives in wartime to act as ambulance units at the thick of the battle.

☐ Can you name any other Christian pacifist group?

The nuclear threat

Since World War II, people have been faced with a terrible dilemma since an entirely new situation has arisen. Nuclear weapons could destroy life as we know it on this planet. By 1984 we already had enough nuclear weapons to wipe out humanity forty times over. No one wants to be annihilated by nuclear war so the best way to keep the peace and reduce the number of weapons is hotly argued. Here are some options.

Women at Greenham Common, 1982. The first aim of the Greenham women was to persuade the UK to reject American Cruise Missiles.

Unilateralism

Unilateralists in this country want Britain to get rid of all its nuclear weapons immediately, without waiting for arms agreements. This would be a first step to nuclear disarmament by all countries. They regard the presence of cruise missiles as a great danger for this country, and say that the British government cannot actually prevent their use. (The Conservative party, however, states that any decision on their use would be taken jointly by the British and United States governments.) Many would like Western Europe to declare itself a nuclear-free zone without waiting for arms agreements between the USA and the USSR.

Some unilateralists stress the need for nuclear disarmament but also believe that we need strong **conventional forces** (non-nuclear) to keep law and order in the world, so as to protect weak nations from possible exploitation.

Multilateralism

Some Westerners believe that the USSR is a very aggressive power. They point to its invasions of Hungary and Afghanistan and the lack of individual freedom in Communist countries. These people believe the only way to keep the peace is to have sufficient nuclear arms to ward off any possible threat (**deterrence**). If the West were weak, they say, it would be prey to blackmail and eventual takeover. So the West must negotiate arms control and eventual disarmament from a position of strength, which gives greater bargaining power. This is the multilateral approach.

Other people believe the USA is equally aggressive. They mention American policy in Latin America, its invasion of Grenada and support for Nicaraguan rebels as examples. These people want both sides to see the folly of their present attitudes; while East and West try to keep up with each other's nuclear potential, the weapons become more sophisticated and terrible.

☐ What is meant by *peace education* in schools? Should it be part of the school curriculum?

☐ What basic facts and figures about the nuclear debate do you know? Or is the topic so horrible that you feel you don't want to know?

A Costa Rican village health centre. Costa Rica abolished its army in 1949. Much of the money no longer used for weapons has gone to health and education.

Infant deaths and malnutrition have fallen sharply and life expectancy has risen to 70 years.

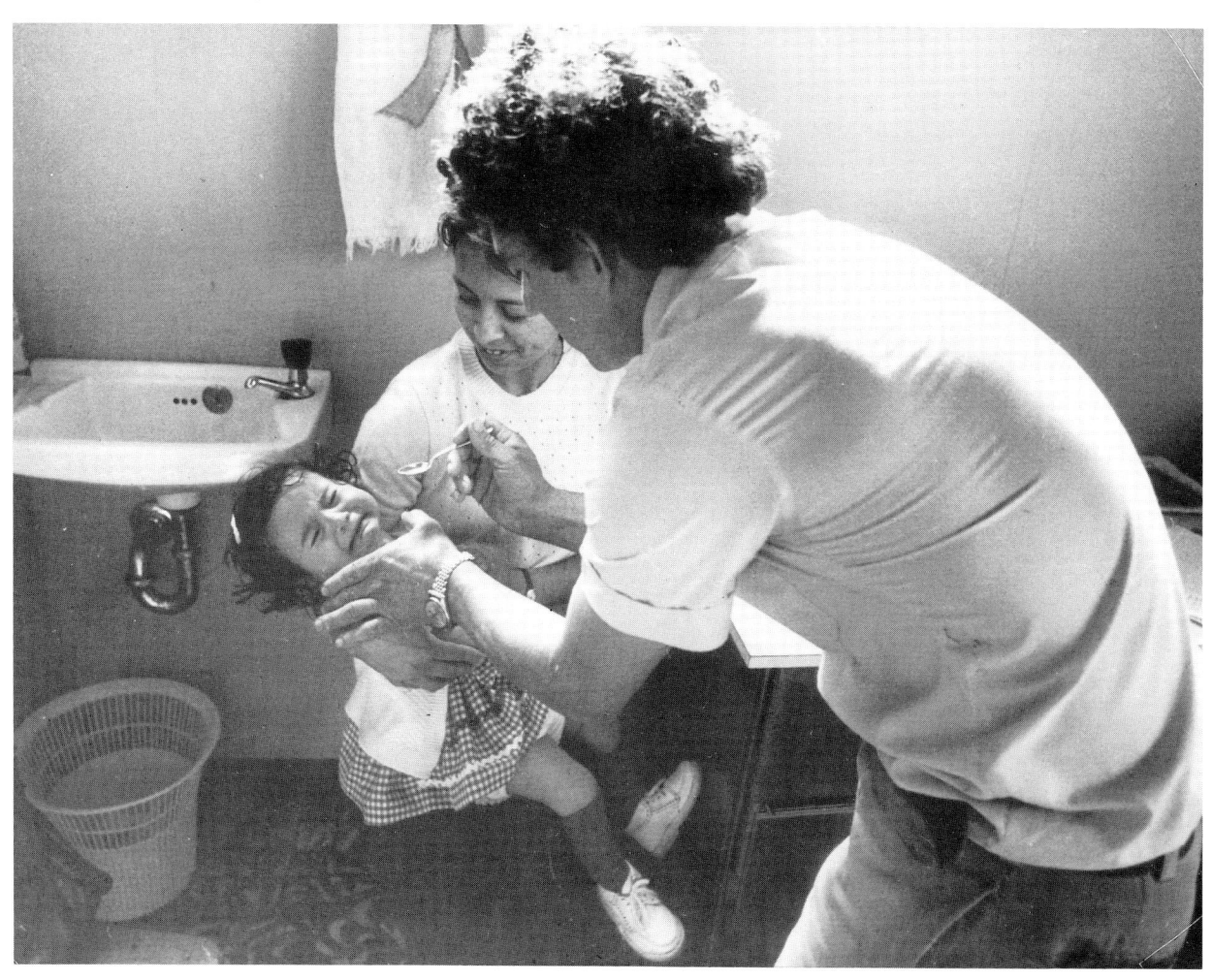

The arms race and the war machine

Between 1960 and 1982 nearly 11 million people died in 65 wars fought in 49 countries – a rate of 1,330 dead every day for 22 years. These appalling statistics show why arms manufacture is a big and profitable business. The USA, USSR, France, Italy, Israel and Britain are amongst the most successful arms traders.

> ☐ Where are wars being fought at the moment? What are their causes?

Global military spending is running at over one million dollars *per minute*, equal to 110 dollars for every man, woman and child on earth. Worldwide military spending averages 19,300 dollars per soldier compared with public education of 380 dollars per school-age child.

Large sums of money are also spent on research into new weapons. For example in the UK in 1982, 53 per cent of the research and development budget was actually spent on war-related topics. Approximately half our scientists and engineers are busy making more efficient missiles, planes, ships and other military objects. To put it another way, in 1982 the average British family spent £18 a week on arms.

The fact that so much money is spent on military research means that there is much less available for medical and non-military scientific projects. This applies throughout the world. The United Nations Committee for Development and Planning (1980) declared:

> The single and most massive obstacle to development is the world-wide expenditure on national defence activity.

In 1980 the global expenditure on military research was more than the *total* amount spent on energy, health, pollution control and agriculture.

> ☐ *'In the arms race there will be no winners, only a dead heat.'* Discuss what kind of a dead heat the writer has in mind. What picture would you use to illustrate this saying?

Over to you

a) Read Isaiah 2:3–4. Write a poem or a short essay describing in modern terms the vision of a peaceful world which this prophet saw.

b) Write out the verses which include Jesus' teaching on this topic: Matthew 5:9, 21–2, 38–9, 43–4; 7:1, 12.

c) Do a project on the controversial life of the German Pastor Martin Niemoeller, a 'militant pacifist' who died aged 92 in March 1984,

OR the aims and achievements of the Greenham Common women. Look carefully at the arguments used against them by some Newbury residents. Discuss also the comment, *'They are the conscience of us all.'*

d) Discuss the following: *'Arms are not the real threat to peace. The real threat lies in the fear or hostility of nations and in aggression itself.'*

e) *'In the event of a nuclear war there will be no chances and there will be no survivors – all will be obliterated'* – Lord Louis Mountbatten. Who was Lord Mountbatten? Why should his words be taken seriously?

f) Discuss the claim that *'The most effective civil defence is to work for peace among nations.'*

Find out what you can about the many different kinds of peace groups at work and the variety of people involved in them.

21 The World Community

One of the most dramatic pictures to appear on our television screens in 1984 was that of the American astronaut moving alone in space, away from his craft, silhouetted starkly against the backcloth of planet earth. The scientific achievements of this century have been extraordinary, particularly in the area of telecommunications. We can now have instant news of events around the world, from the funeral of a Soviet leader to the election of a United States President. We can forget the vast distances which separate us when we are able to speak to someone half-way across the world.

> ☐ Suppose you had close relatives living in Tokyo, Melbourne, Capetown, Leningrad and Jerusalem. Work out what time you would have to put in a telephone call in order to speak to them at 9 a.m. on their birthdays.

World citizenship

For the first time in human history we now have a world organisation, the **United Nations**, which since its beginning in 1945 has dedicated itself to three things:

1 To keep world peace and security.

2 To fight against poverty, hunger and illiteracy.

3 To help all people gain basic human rights and freedoms.

Almost every nation of the world is now a member of the UN and has signed its Charter, which begins:

> We the peoples of the United Nations [are] determined... to practise tolerance and live together in peace with one another as good neighbours...

The United Kingdom was a founder member of the UN and is one of the five permanent members of the **Security Council**. All member states belong to the **General Assembly**.

Several self-governing international organisations are associated with the UN (see below) and working alongside the UN agencies there are many voluntary organisations such as Oxfam, Christian Aid, Save the Children Fund and War on Want (see Resources section).

We are beginning to realise, therefore, that we need to become good citizens not only of our own local community and national society but also of the world. And one of the first steps in citizenship is to learn about some of the basic problems facing us all today and how we can contribute to their solutions.

The problems of the world

Limited resources

Our beautiful planet earth has its limits. The sea takes up 70 per cent of the world's surface and only about 18 per cent of the remaining mass can adequately support normal human life. The rest consists either of ice or semi-arid or arid (dry) deserts. Humanity has not yet learnt to care for its fertile soil. In the 'developed' world (the rich, industrialised countries) millions of acres of fertile land are swallowed up each year by the needs of housing, transport and industrial development. Yet we know that it takes a thousand years of natural growth to produce only two inches of good top soil. And in 'developing' countries, land is lost to the desert each year. This may happen through neglect or it may be that people's immediate needs force them to sacrifice the long-term good, so they do not let the land lie fallow for a period, and thus it deteriorates.

Also in this century humanity is using enormous quantities of fuel for energy. Oil, coal, natural gas and minerals are global resources which we cannot renew. Unless the world community combines to conserve resources, supplies of non-renewable energy will cease.

The Environment

We need to realise that human beings do not own the world. We share this planet with other living creatures and with plant and vegetable life. In this century human beings have done appalling damage to the environment – the seas, the rivers, the land and air. Many kinds of wildlife and priceless natural areas are threatened with extinction. There are now, however, hopeful signs that the world community is beginning to see that conservation is absolutely necessary to our survival.

Over-population

At one time the world had a more or less static population of about 200 million people who lived mainly through agriculture. Old age was rare and more than half the children born did not survive to become parents themselves. Since the eighteenth century all this has changed through the great improvements in medicine, hygiene and general standards of living. World population is estimated at about 4,800 billion (1984) and will probably reach about seven billion in AD 2000 (a billion is a thousand million).

Many of the rich countries have encouraged people to limit their families through birth control methods so that their population has now become relatively stable. In the UK, for example, it stays around the 55 million mark. But families in the 'Third World' either cannot or do not want to limit the number of children they have because of poverty, insecurity about the future, lack of education and lack of basic information about birth control methods or means to buy them.

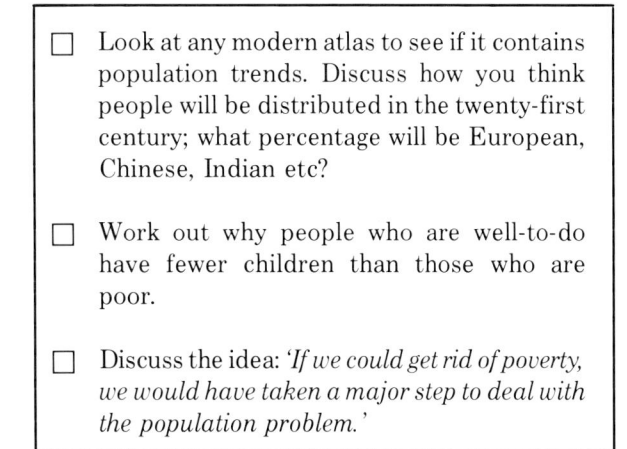

- ☐ Look at any modern atlas to see if it contains population trends. Discuss how you think people will be distributed in the twenty-first century; what percentage will be European, Chinese, Indian etc?

- ☐ Work out why people who are well-to-do have fewer children than those who are poor.

- ☐ Discuss the idea: *'If we could get rid of poverty, we would have taken a major step to deal with the population problem.'*

Bob Geldof visiting Mali for Band Aid in 1985. He has brought famine in Africa to world attention and has made people aware that famines are not only caused by natural disasters but also by human greed and selfishness.

Poverty, health, education, development

In this century the world's economy has developed very unequally. There is a great division between the rich, developed, industrialised countries known as the **North** where 30 per cent of the world population lives and the underdeveloped or developing countries known as the **South** or **Third World**, containing 70 per cent of humanity.

One fifth of humanity lives in absolute poverty and 500 million are unemployed. There is a continual drift from rural areas as people seek work in the cities, often a hopeless search. This movement of population is creating vast new sprawling slums and squatter settlements.

It is estimated that 15 million under-fives die each year. Yet at least 90 per cent of these deaths could have been prevented by the provision of clean water and adequate sanitation. For the same reasons, an equal number of children suffer either physical or mental handicap. There is also widespread illiteracy.

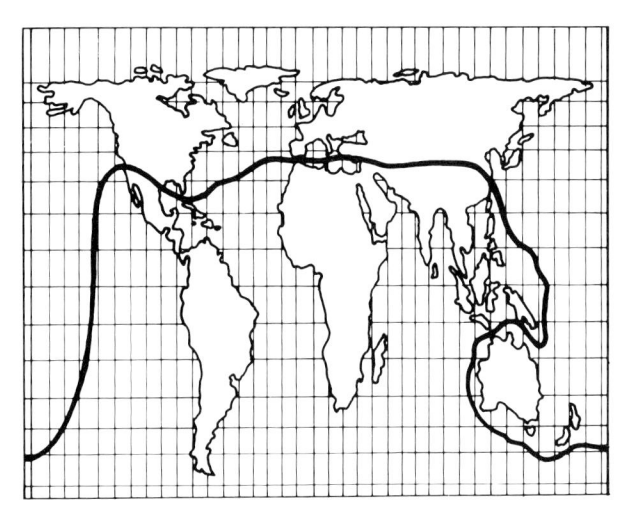

The Brandt Report divided the world into the poor South and the rich North, as shown below and above the line.

The work of the United Nations

Since the UN was formed, it has successfully helped to keep some sixty local wars within limits.

We tend to think of it only as a peacekeeper, because wars are headline news, but the UN is involved in almost every important aspect of human life. Besides running many permanent organisations, it also works for particular groups of people from time to time. There was International Women's Year in 1975, International Year of the Child in 1979, of the Disabled in 1981, of Youth in 1985. Briefly:

FAO is the Food and Agricultural Organisation: it aims to raise the level of nutrition throughout the world and prevent world hunger. When a drought or famine crisis arises, the FAO together with other agencies tries to deal with the situation.

ILO is the International Labour Organisation: it aims to improve working conditions in the world and has set up an International Labour Code on many aspects of labour such as the employment of women and children. In 1976 it launched a World Employment Programme.

UNESCO is the UN Educational, Scientific and Cultural Organisation. One of its aims is to establish primary school education throughout the world and to raise the level of adult literacy. In the 1960s it sent educational experts to 21 countries in response to government requests.

WHO, the World Health Organisation, works to promote the highest possible level of health. Over a period of ten years it succeeded in getting rid of smallpox.

UNICEF is the UN Children's Emergency Fund; it works with WHO to help governments improve mother and child care, aiming to help children in need. It believes that educating girls and women is one of the surest ways of not only

A tube well in Bangladesh. UNICEF calls for 'clean water and adequate sanitation for all', to save millions of lives.

cutting child deaths in the developing world, but also controlling the birth rate. At first many areas opposed the idea of female education but over the past twenty years great progress has been made in many countries.

UNFPA is the UN Fund for Population Activities which was set up to help with population problems. In 1984 an International Conference was held in Mexico to discuss population trends.

UNHCR, the UN High Commission for Refugees, seeks to protect the legal rights of well over ten million refugees throughout the world. It works with the voluntary agencies to help provide them with food, shelter and new homes.

The UN has also sponsored conferences on trade and development, science and technology, and many other issues of world importance. For example, in 1979 at the UN Conference on Trade and Development (UNCTAD Five), 'North' and 'South' representatives discussed sharing the planet's resources more evenly and providing equal opportunity for developing them.

What we can do

1 Become well informed about different parts of the world, and especially about the basic inequalities between 'North' and 'South'.

2 Support one or more of the many agencies at work, either through fundraising or by telling others about their activities.

3 Start a UN Association branch at school so that you can keep in touch with the many aspects of its work.

4 Support the British Volunteer programme which consists of four organisations sending volunteers to developing countries.

5 Support One World Week, held in October each year. It was begun by the World Development Movement and is sponsored by Christian Aid and many churches (see the Resources section).

Christian and Jewish attitudes

The Jew and Christian see the whole universe as God's creation (Genesis 1). Humanity has been given the power to rule, especially over the animal kingdom. But we must use this authority for the glory of God, not selfishly. Many Christians therefore feel deep concern and commitment for world problems.

Over to you

a) Read Psalm 8:3–9 and Psalm 104:5, 24. Write out the two verses from Psalm 104.

b) Look up Leviticus 25:18–38. The writer is saying that as the land belongs to God, the rich should not buy it for ever.
Discuss the situation of the 600 million destitute and landless people in the world in the light of these verses.

c) Do a project on one of the UN agencies or one of the charitable organisations such as Save the Children Fund, or War on Want.

d) Write out the last verse of James 2:14–17. Discuss the importance of the whole passage for this section.

e) Do a project on one of the conservation organisations such as the World Wildlife Fund, the Conservation Society or Friends of the Earth.

f) Discuss what Jacques Cousteau meant when he said, *'We have the remedies on the shelf, and the only question is whether we will use them.'*

g) E.F. Schumacher, the author of *Small is Beautiful*, believed that very simple designs, local materials and local workers were more useful than imported 'high technology' in supporting developing countries to help themselves. He called his system Intermediate Technology. Christian Aid, Oxfam and other groups operating in Third World countries are finding these comparatively inexpensive, small scale units very successful in their work. Do a project on Intermediate Technology.

22 Suffering

Pain is a fact of life whether it is physical, emotional or mental. In this country we are lucky. Most of us are healthier than our ancestors and therefore more of us live physically pain-free and longer lives. In the more deprived areas of the world, millions of people are less fortunate.

Some physical pain is a necessary warning that our bodies are not working as well as they ought to be or that we are misusing them in some way. Toothache is one example and sickness after over-eating is another.

- [ ] Can you think of further examples?

Inflicted pain

Then there is the pain which is caused by other people. As human beings we know the difference between a good thought, word and deed and a bad one. We can choose to be helpful, considerate, kind and honest or the reverse. And other people either benefit or are hurt by what we say and do. A great deal of suffering in the world is brought about by totally selfish and irresponsible behaviour.

- [ ] Look at any newspaper and find examples of some completely undeserved hurt or disaster which has been caused by cruelty, greed or irresponsibility, as for example when an old age pensioner is robbed of his/her savings.

In certain parts of the world, people suffer because they live under oppressive and unjust regimes. They may be tortured and imprisoned because of their political or religious beliefs.

- [ ] Discuss whether it is ever right to inflict pain on people to make them 'confess'.

Ignorance

In the past, the basic cause of illness or accident was often lack of knowledge. During the Middle Ages, for example, great plagues swept through Europe because people did not understand the effects of bad drains and untreated sewage. We still do not know enough to be sure what will result from certain actions. Sometimes new drugs have to be taken off the market because they are found to have harmful side-effects in spite of passing experimental tests satisfactorily.

- [ ] Do you know anything about the thalidomide babies? Ask your parents or people of their age group to tell you about them.

- [ ] What other examples can you think of in ordinary everyday life where ignorance causes suffering? You might remember incidents from your own childhood!

Natural disasters

Throughout the world there are areas where volcanoes erupt, tornadoes devastate, the earth quakes, the sun scorches, there is too little rain or too much and people are made homeless, maimed or killed by these natural disasters. No one is actually to blame for these catastrophes although sometimes the rest of the world does not do enough to bring comfort and support to the sufferers. Scientific knowledge, especially meteorology (weather forecasting), can often warn the area of possible disaster but very poor countries cannot afford or benefit from expensive technology.

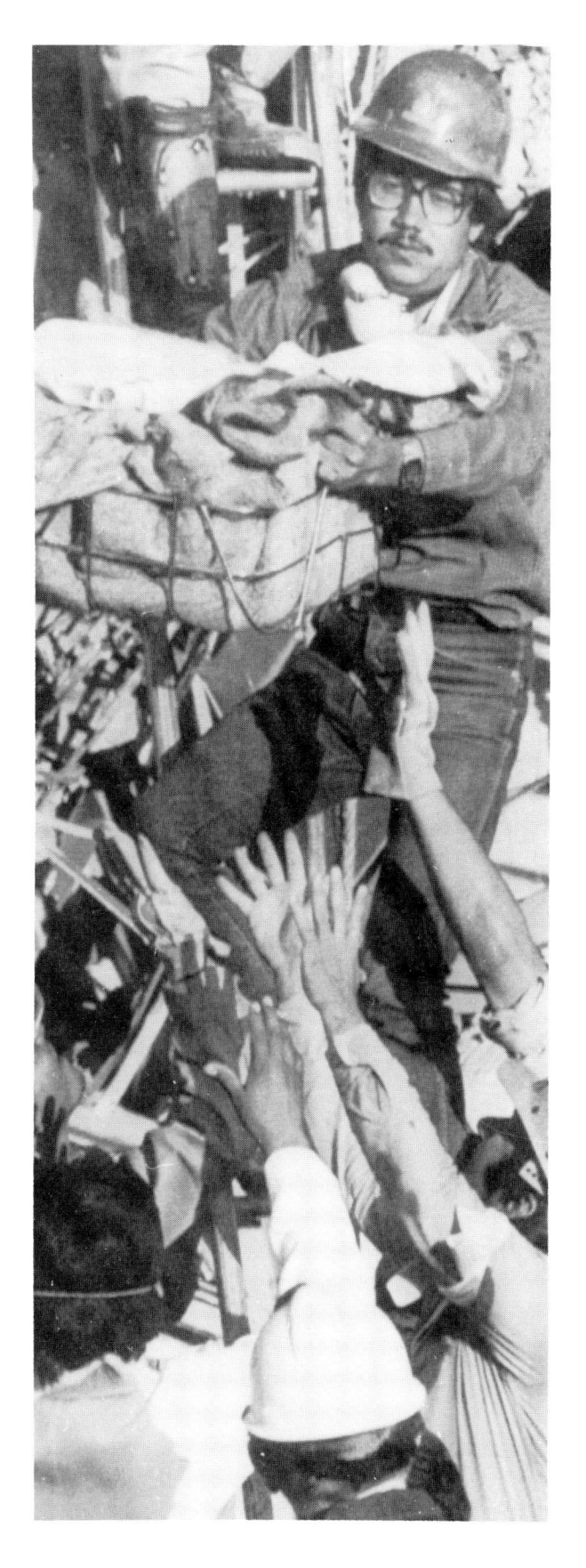

☐ Can you name regions in the world today where people are experiencing hardship through natural calamities? What is being done to bring relief to them?

Undeserved suffering

We are all part of the human family therefore we suffer with, because, and for each other whether we like it or not. Totally undeserved suffering such as an unexpected and crippling accident or illness is difficult to bear, but people's courage and faith in such circumstances helps all of us.

☐ What do you know about Pat Seed? How did her courage help thousands of other people? (See Further Reading section.)

Biblical views

People have always asked one basic question about suffering: If God is good and all-powerful, why does he allow it to happen?

One answer to this difficult problem is as follows: Although God is at work in his world bringing about his good purposes, he does not force his will on human beings. He has given

Baby rescued alive from the Mexican earthquake 1985. Natural disasters are often made worse by human error or greed; many parts of Mexico City were not built to stand severe stress, yet earthquakes often happen there.

them free will because they will only learn to grow and take responsibility for each other and their planet when they exercise freedom of choice.

This does not explain natural disasters but many modern Christians believe that our planet is governed by its own laws, and that humanity is constantly being challenged to discover them.

The Bible has many things to say about the problem of suffering. Here are three:

1 It gives the vision and hope of a world made free from unnecessary pain and conflict (Isaiah 11:6–9).

2 Although humans inflict pain upon each other either through careless selfishness or evil motives, God can somehow use all this for good purposes (Genesis 50:20).

3 Some people are loving and unselfish enough to suffer for the sake of others. When they freely accept suffering which they have not deserved, their unselfishness can bring relief and release for countless others (Isaiah 53:4–9). Jesus is the supreme example of this attitude.

Modern examples

1 The ideal of the welfare state is to create a society which cares for those in need. It aims to lessen suffering as much as possible, even though the state cannot take away all the causes of pain.

2 Accidents at work and on the roads are in themselves evil. On the other hand, popular concern about such suffering has led to better laws and safety regulations, so that a general improvement has been achieved.

3 Courageous people have freely risked their lives to bring help and comfort to others. This is especially true of diseases such as leprosy and cancer. Thanks to the willing sacrifice of these individuals, humanity has gained knowledge which has benefited us all.

☐ Can you think of other examples?

Over to you

a) Read Isaiah 11:6–9. Isaiah lived about seven hundred years before Jesus. During his lifetime his country went through many political crises but through his faith in God he could look forward to a future time of peace and blessedness, like the Paradise pictured in Genesis 2.

Draw or paint some of the situations he describes.

b) You will probably know the long story about Joseph and his brothers (Genesis 37, 40, 41, 45). Its theme is that goodness can come out of evil if a man has courage and faith in God.

Write a short essay either about Joseph or about a modern situation in which evil is turned to good account.

c) Read Isaiah 53:4–9. The prophet was writing about the servant of God. Although innocent himself, he was willing to accept punishment which the guilty deserved. Jesus must have thought deeply on this theme. He warned his disciples that he would probably have to die for his convictions (Mark 8:31), but he believed God would work through him to restore other people (Mark 10:45).

d) Discuss the idea of suffering for the sake of others, for example a mother for her child, a father for his family, a friend for friend, a patriot for his/her country.

e) Find out what you can about Sheila Cassidy – a doctor who worked in Chile. In what sense did she come to believe that suffering brought her closer to God?

Do a project on the life of either Sheila Cassidy or Pat Seed.

23 Breaking Free

Old Testament views

Human beings are very complex. We can be guided by both good and bad impulses. The Old Testament writers saw wrong-doing or sin as the outcome of a bad impulse and defined it as an action which broke one of God's laws. They thought sin was punished in one of two ways: either God would strike the sinner with some tragedy or illness, or the community would deal out justice. For example, the commandment 'You shall not kill' (Exodus 20:13) was followed by the punishment 'the murderer shall be put to death' (Numbers 35:16).

Culprits were punished for wrong-doing so that they would understand their misdeeds and would feel sorry for having done them. It was a way of ensuring that they did not repeat the sin, either because they feared further consequences or because they were truly sorry. The well-being of the community was all-important, so evils such as murder were more harshly dealt with than others.

A moral law in the universe

Experience tells us, however, that some people 'get away' with evil. They are not found out and therefore escape punishment. But the biblical writers are clear that wrong-doing is not only hurtful to others but is self-destructive as well. Paul put it this way (Galatians 6:7):

> Do not be deceived; God is not mocked, for whatever a man sows, that he will reap.

In other words, even though wrong-doers appear to be escaping the consequences of their actions, it is really not so. By breaking certain basic moral laws they are degrading and destroying themselves as human beings. Look at the case of a man who consistently tells lies. In the end he cannot tell truth from falsehood. People eventually discover his dishonesty and no longer trust him. He loses their respect and friendship. He has made himself poorer by his deceit.

☐ Can you think of other examples of self-destructive behaviour? Think about addiction.

Punishment is not enough

Punishment alone has not solved the problem of wrong-doing. Passing and enforcing laws does not always make people good. People also need to have a strong inner belief in doing what is right. One person may only tell the truth because he/she is afraid of the consequences if caught lying. Another may believe sincerely that honesty is the best policy. The first one is far more likely than the second to fall into the temptation to deceive if it suits his/her purpose.

☐ Can you think of other examples?

Finding an answer to sin

Jesus said in effect that he had come to cure the sickness of sin (Mark 2:13–17). Part of that cure was that people should learn to understand their own motives. The old law forbade killing, but

In Rome's Rebibba gaol, Pope John Paul II talks to Mehmet Ali Agca who tried to murder him in 1981.

Pope John Paul felt no bitterness towards the would-be assassin.

Jesus forbade hatred and anger. He saw that if these feelings were not controlled they could lead in the end to murderous thoughts and actions (Matthew 5:21–2).

For the second part of the cure, people had to be willing to forgive and be forgiven (Mark 11:25). This would release the power of compassionate love (Matthew 5:44–5):

> 'Love your enemies and pray for those who persecute you, so that you may be sons of your Father who is in heaven.'

He was saying that retaliation only makes matters worse.

☐ Discuss how this happens, looking at Northern Ireland as your example.

The third part of the cure happened when people recognised that the power to love all stemmed from God. Jesus believed that his own relationship with God was all-important. He himself did not give way to hatred. Even when he was dying in agony, his enemies could not crush his compassion and his willingness to forgive them (Luke 23:34).

Freedom

Jesus was free from self-concern. He never took the attitude, 'I want this for myself, therefore I must have it.' He was full of concern for others. And his disciples, through faith in him, felt this same powerful freedom in their lives. Paul could write to his friends, 'Do not be overcome by evil, but overcome evil with good' (Romans 12:21), even though he had experienced many terrible things for his faith (2 Corinthians 11:24–9).

Therefore the follower of Jesus believes that the individual has found true freedom when compassion and tenderness are stronger than indifference and cruelty. Goodness is a positive, creative and liberating force, whereas evil is negative, destructive and crippling (John 8:34):

> 'Everyone who commits sin is a slave to sin. The slave does not continue in the house for ever; the son continues for ever. So if the Son makes you free, you will be free indeed.'

Discuss the following:

☐ *'Getting to know the truth about oneself is an important step towards real freedom.'*

☐ *'Selfishness imprisons; Love liberates.'*

☐ *'Love makes you vulnerable. The only way to be free is to be independent.'*

☐ *'If you love enough, even through hurt and harm, you can be free because you are not tied by bitterness or resentment.'*

Over to you

a) Look up Jeremiah 31:31–4. The prophet dreamt of a time when his people would have a new relationship with God. In that new age, his laws would be written in their hearts. They would continually choose to do right from firm belief, not from fear.

Discuss our need for a change of heart, a change of outlook, a new approach in the modern world.

b) Read Mark 2:13–17. Jesus had just asked the tax collector Levi to be his friend and disciple. He was having dinner with him, much to the horror of the scribes and Pharisees. They believed a good person would obey all the religious rules to the last detail and they looked on sin (i.e. breaking the rules) almost as an infectious disease. If you came in contact with a sinner (and a tax collector was certainly that) you could become defiled or religiously unclean. So they were critical of Jesus for the company he kept.

Jesus answered them in their own terms by quoting a proverb. In Jesus' view the law of God was the law of love, not a matter of ritual regulations. Therefore he saw sin as the unloving thought, word or action of which all are guilty. He saw that all people needed what he had to give, including the scribes and Pharisees, even though they did not realise it.

c) How would you define sin? Discuss what real goodness means. Why is it mistaken to connect it with boring behaviour, conformity or excessive meekness?

d) Read 2 Corinthians 11:24–9 to see what Paul went through for his faith. Write down his words in Romans 12:21.

e) When Martin Luther King was assassinated in 1968, his wife, Coretta, said that she forgave his murderer. How difficult do you think this was for her? What freedom did she gain by doing so?

f) Write a short story in which someone overcomes evil with good, in the way that Pope John Paul II forgave his would-be assassin.

24 Fulfilment

It is one thing to want to be kind and honest in all our dealings with other people. It is another to have the strength and the willpower to do it. Paul knew all about this conflict when he wrote in his letter to the Romans (7:18–19):

> I can will what is right, but I cannot do it. For I do not do the good I want, but the evil I do not want is what I do.

He believed that it was sin within himself which prevented him from fulfilling his best intentions. He found the answer to the problem through faith in Jesus (Romans 8:2):

> For the law of the Spirit of life in Christ Jesus has set me free from the law of sin and death.

The basis of the religious life therefore is that people are not alone in their dilemmas. God is the source of life and love. Prayer and worship are essential for well-being. Through prayer people can develop a deeper relationship with God. With this inner power and strength people can learn to live rightly.

> ☐ Discuss the statement: *'We cannot treat God like a slot machine, popping in a prayer and expecting the equivalent of a bar of chocolate or a cup of coffee in return, without any effort on our part.'*

What is prayer?

The Christian will look to Jesus both as an example and a teacher about prayer. He taught his disciples that it was sincerity that mattered, not the words used or the length of time spent in the outward forms of praying (Matthew 6:6):

> 'When you pray, go into your room and shut the door and pray to your Father who is in secret; and your Father who sees in secret will reward you.'

God knows all the needs of people before they express them. Nevertheless, by putting their needs into words people learn more about themselves. Prayer is communion or inner conversation with God (or Jesus), of the sort we would have with a close friend.

Although at times it is hard to understand how God answers prayer, Jesus was quite clear that real prayer is never wasted. At their request, he taught his disciples a simple pattern of prayer based on his own experience of the Fatherhood of God (Luke 11:1–4). The gospels show that Jesus himself spent much time praying (Mark 1:35) and stressed the power of prayer. On one occasion when his disciples were unable to heal he told them they had not prayed enough (Mark 9:14–29).

Luke records one of Jesus' humorous stories, the Friend at Midnight, to show that God cares deeply for people, even more than the best of parents. People are to ask, seek and knock, for God will always respond. But requests and seeking are to lead to the Kingdom, not to selfish ends (Luke 11:5–13).

When Jesus was in terrible conflict about his forthcoming arrest and probable death, he prayed that God might find a way for him to avoid the agony ahead. Then, as his prayer deepened, he became able to accept whatever the future held (Mark 14:32–42). Obviously he gained great strength from that time in the Garden of Gethsemane; when evil and torment later descended upon him, his spirit of love was not overcome (Luke 23:34–43).

> ☐ A daughter and son may pray frequently and with deep sincerity for their mother to recover from a serious illness, and yet she dies; or that their father will get a job, yet he remains unemployed. Discuss what good might come from such prayers, even if what was asked for does not happen.

Worship

Jesus quoted verses from Deuteronomy and Leviticus when he summarised the whole of the Jewish law (Deuteronomy 6:4–5; see Mark 12:28–30):

> 'Hear, O Israel: The LORD our God is one LORD; and you shall love the LORD your God with all your heart, and with all your soul, and with all your might.'

Worship is an essential part of life for Jew and Christian alike and worship does not only consist of private prayer and meditation. It also means coming together as a family or community to give praise and thanksgiving.

Luke tells us a little about the early Christians in Jerusalem. Sometimes they met in the home of Mary, the mother of John Mark (Acts 12:12), but they also attended the Temple services (2:43–7). They kept the Jewish Sabbath but gradually the first day of the week (Sunday), which had special meaning for them because of Jesus' resurrection, became their main meeting day (Acts 20:7–12).

In the twentieth century, Christian worship expresses itself in a variety of ways and the Church today is split up into many different **denominations** (separate Christian Churches).

> ☐ How many can you name?

All denominations base their forms of worship on their own interpretation of the New Testament. For example, although most Christians believe in infant baptism, when a baby is brought by its parents to be received into the Christian family, there are some Christians (Baptists) who only hold a believer's baptism (i.e. when someone is old enough to make a personal decision) while others (Quakers) do not see the need for any baptism at all.

> ☐ Discuss some of the different forms of worship which take place in, for instance, a Roman Catholic or a Methodist church.

At one time, Christians were so deeply divided and so critical of each other's approach that they fought wars to gain power and to compel others to accept their way of worship. Now there is much better understanding and tolerance and the ecumenical movement to unite all churches is growing. (*Ecumenical* is from a Greek word which means the inhabited earth.)

> ☐ Is there a Council of Churches in your neighbourhood, where members of different denominations meet and worship together?

Fulfilment

In John's gospel (10:10) Jesus directly says:

> 'I came that they may have life, and have it abundantly.'

And it is clear that he was not only talking about eternal life but about the here and now. The word *gospel* means 'good news'. The first Christians saw the coming of Jesus as the good news for all humanity. Through him men and women could once more find the right relationship with God and with each other, a relationship based on forgiveness, reconciliation, love and trust.

The beginning of the Sermon on the Mount (Matthew 5:3–12) is known as the Beatitudes; *blessed*, the word Jesus repeats nine times, means happy. At first these nine statements about the happy person seem completely untrue to life, but Jesus is saying that these are the

Christians from many denominations celebrating Easter at an ecumenical gathering at Taize' (France).

qualities which will give a person the right relationship with God. It is this which brings inner peace, even if there is also suffering. For Jesus, the way of happiness is to be aware not only of self but also of others, and, above all, of God. For him, worldly success was not important and aggression was useless. He believed instead in the value of justice, mercy and compassion. Later in the Sermon, Jesus stressed the importance of right motive. He also warned that the love of money is dangerous. Material things must be kept in their right place, otherwise people become fearful and anxious about losing what they have.

Although Paul at first persecuted the emerging Christian Church, he had an overwhelming experience which convinced him that Jesus had indeed risen from the dead and was the Son of God. This transformed his life. He sometimes used the expression that he had 'put on the Lord Jesus Christ' (Romans 13:14) or 'put on love' (Colossians 3:12, 14) to describe the complete change in his life.

In Acts, Luke shows how Jesus' early disciples had a great sense of peace and fellowship with each other. Even persecution and death by martyrdom could not destroy their joy. This has also been the experience of millions of believers down the centuries. The challenge for Christians today is to show how the way of love, peace, reconciliation, service and joy brings real personal fulfilment.

- How would you define happiness?
- Discuss the differences between the *pleasure* of eating a good meal, job *satisfaction* and the *joy* of being reunited with someone you love. Think of other examples for each category.

Over to you

a) The psalms are individual or communal prayers. Look up Psalm 25:4–10. Discuss the theme of the prayer.

b) Read Luke 18:1–14 where Jesus tells two parables about prayer. In the first he says that if an unjust human judge can be persuaded to deal with a poor widow's case, even against his selfish will, how much more will God deal justly. In the second he contrasts the attitude of a self-satisfied Pharisee with that of a sinful tax collector who asks forgiveness because he knows that his life is corrupt.

Discuss modern equivalents to the two men and their approach to God.

c) Look up Acts 20:7–12 and role play the scene.

d) Do a project on the rites and worship of one Christian denomination about which you know very little at present,

OR on the World Council of Churches.

e) Write out 1 Corinthians 12:12–13 and put in your own words what these verses say about Christian unity.

f) Read Romans 12:9–18. Make a list of the things that Paul believed added up to a good life.

Compare this with what Jesus said in Matthew 5:3–10.

Write down your own definition of a good life.

25 Death and Eternity

Suicide

In this country there is a low death rate amongst babies and children and most of us can expect to survive for seventy or more years. Nevertheless it is a harsh comment on our society that each year hundreds of people take their own lives and many more try to do so. Sometimes people commit suicide because they are mentally ill and are suffering from acute depression; sometimes it is because they are desperately lonely or cannot face the future; sometimes it is because of a terrible incurable disease.

Often the attempted suicide is stating in actions rather than words the despair he/she feels in having no one to turn to in a crisis.

Jewish and Christian attitudes

Some ancient and modern societies have considered that taking one's own life can be an honourable thing to do. Jews and Christians, on the contrary, believe that all life is sacred and belongs to God. Therefore they see suicide in almost the same light as murder, since both mean taking away life. So they are deeply concerned to help anyone who is struggling with the temptation to 'end it all'.

The Samaritans organisation, for example, was founded in 1953 by an Anglican priest, Chad Varah. When Samaritans are actually helping people, however, they make no attempt to convert would-be suicides to any religious belief. In fact many of the trained volunteers who work for Samaritans in their centres throughout the country are not necessarily members of any religious group.

> ☐ Discuss some of the reasons which might lead a person to think of suicide.
>
> ☐ Discuss also this statement: *'If a person who thought of suicide lived in a caring community, the chances are that matters could be sorted out before things went very badly wrong.'*

Euthanasia

This word means arranging for a person who is suffering from an agonising, incurable condition to die quickly and with as little difficulty as possible.

We may all of us feel dread at the prospect of a horrible and lingering death. Provided we could retain our faculties, we would probably all prefer to die peacefully of old age. But we know from experience that this does not always happen. Some people therefore think we have the right to make our own choices about dying with dignity. Those wanting to legalise euthanasia say that if they develop an incurable disease they do not want their life to be prolonged 'unnecessarily'. Nor do they want to be kept on a life-support machine if they have no hope of conscious survival.

For obvious reasons, however, doctors are reluctant to predict definitely how long any patient may live and at the present time it is a serious criminal offence to aid, advise or bring about anyone else's suicide or voluntary death.

Samaritans listen warmly, patiently and sympathetically to anyone in need. They can be of any age, religion, race or sex.

- ☐ Discuss the difference between voluntary and compulsory euthanasia (as happened under the Nazi regime).

- ☐ Discuss the terrible dilemma which faces parents if their child has been injured in a road accident and suffers severe brain damage, being kept alive only on a support machine. Should they agree to its being turned off?

Hospices for the dying

There is another way to deal with the incurably ill and to ease both their suffering and that of their relatives. Hospices have been founded which are specially organised to care for terminally ill patients. Dame Cicely Saunders started the first hospice in London in the 1960s. Since then others have been built in various parts of the country.

These hospices are supported by a great deal of voluntary work. In the peaceful, caring atmosphere of the hospice where everyone knows openly that the illness is terminal, the patients are encouraged to live as fully as they can. Drug therapy keeps them as free from pain as possible and sometimes they may even recover sufficiently to go home.

Life after death

Some of the earliest relics of ancient people show how they buried their dead with care and with provisions for some future life. Belief in survival after death is found in practically all religions, and is very strongly held by Christians.

In Jesus' day the Pharisees believed in resurrection from the dead, but only for those who had been faithful to God. The wicked would go to Sheol – the underworld – a place of shadowy non-existence.

The Sadducees, the high priestly class, believed that you only survived through your descendants. (That was why it was so important to have children to carry on your name.) They asked Jesus a trick question about the afterlife (Mark 12:18–27). In reply he clearly stated his conviction that death is not the end. Life in heaven, however, he said, would be quite different from earthly existence.

Jesus also told his disciples that he believed he would 'rise again' after his death (Mark 8:31; 10:34). And Luke (23:43) says that when Jesus was dying he showed his compassion for the criminal beside him by promising to have fellowship with him in Paradise. In John's Gospel (14:1–3), Jesus assured his friends that life continues beyond the grave.

The Gospels say that Jesus' friends experienced his presence with them three days after his death. We cannot tell what kind of an experience this was, but we do know that it changed their lives. They later received the gift of the Spirit, and the strength of this new-found energy and courage enabled them to travel the Empire preaching the good news of Jesus.

Christians believe that after death they go on to another level of existence where they will be reunited with those they love and will find deeper knowledge of Jesus and God. Jesus' early followers seem to have believed that God's gift of eternal life was only available to those who had faith in Jesus Christ, but only a minority of modern Christians still think that all non-Christians are excluded from life after death. Many also reject the medieval idea that everyone will rise together from the grave on Judgement Day, when the righteous will go to heaven and the wicked to hell.

Some believe that although the human soul or spirit can become immortal, this depends upon the quality of people's lives here on earth. What people do now will equip them (or not) for life hereafter.

The Eastern religions of Hinduism and Buddhism believe in **reincarnation**. This means that through repeated cycles of birth, death and rebirth, people may develop their spiritual life until they eventually find union with the Absolute (God) or the bliss of Nirvana (Heaven).

Islam, like Christianity and certain strands of Judaism, believes that those who have been true to their faith will go on to Paradise.

☐ Do you believe in life after death? Why?

☐ What do you think about the theory of reincarnation? Do you know any people who believe they have had earlier lives in previous centuries? What evidence do they give to support their ideas?

Over to you

a) Do a project on the Samaritans. There is probably a branch in your locality and it might be possible to get someone to come and talk to your group about it.

b) Do a project on the Modern Hospice movement, OR on the work of Cicely Saunders. Find out whether there is a local hospice or support group of people working with the terminally ill.

c) Read the biblical passages quoted in this chapter and discuss their importance for a belief in life after death.

d) Read the following three passages, which are important in helping us to understand Paul's beliefs about life after death: Acts 22:6–11, where Paul describes his vision of Jesus, after Jesus had died; 1 Corinthians 15:3–8, where Paul lists six appearances of the risen Jesus; Philippians 1:19–26, where Paul discusses his own future. He may live longer for the sake of his friends, or he may be executed – but dying has the happy outcome of bringing him closer to Christ.

e) Write out Romans 8:28, 37–9 where Paul expresses his unquenchable faith.

Appendix

Summary of The United Nations Universal Declaration of Human Rights, 1948:

1–3 All human beings are born free and equal in dignity and rights. They are endowed with reason and conscience and should act towards one another in a spirit of brotherhood. Everyone is entitled to all the rights and freedoms set forth in the Declaration without distinction of any kind.... Everyone has the right to life, liberty and security of person.
4 No one shall be held in slavery or servitude...
5 No one shall be subjected to torture or to cruel, inhuman or degrading treatment or punishment.
6 Everyone has the right to recognition everywhere as a person before the law.
7 All are equal before the law...
8 Everyone has the right to an effective remedy by the competent national tribunal for acts violating the fundamental rights granted him by the constitution or by law.
9 No one shall be subjected to arbitrary arrest, detention or exile...
10 Everyone is entitled in full equality to a fair and public hearing...
11 Everyone charged with a penal offence has the right to be presumed innocent until proved guilty...
12 No one shall be subjected to arbitrary interference with his privacy...
13 Everyone has the right to freedom of movement.... Everyone has the right to leave any country...
14 Everyone has the right to seek and to enjoy in other countries asylum from persecution.
15 Everyone has the right to a nationality...
16 Men and women of full age, without any limitation due to race, nationality or religion, have the right to marry and found a family. They are entitled to equal rights as to marriage, during marriage and at its dissolution...
17 Everyone has the right to own property...
18 Everyone has the right to freedom of thought, conscience and religion...
19 Everyone has the right to freedom of opinion and expression...
20 Everyone has the right to freedom of peaceful assembly and association...
21 Everyone has the right to take part in the government of his country, directly or through freely chosen representatives.... The will of the people shall be the basis of the authority of government...
22–3 ... Everyone has the right to work, to free choice of employment, to just and favourable conditions of work and to protection against unemployment...
24 Everyone has the right to rest and leisure...
25 Everyone has the right to a standard of living adequate for health and well-being.... Motherhood and childhood are entitled to special care...
26 Everyone has the right to education.... Education shall be directed to the full development of the human personality and to the strengthening of respect for human rights and fundamental freedoms...
27 Everyone has the right freely to participate in the cultural life of the community...
28 Everyone is entitled to a social and international order in which the rights and freedoms set forth in this Declaration can be fully realized.
29 Everyone has duties to the community...
30 Nothing in this Declaration may be interpreted as implying for any State, group, or person, any right to engage in any activity or to perform any act aimed at the destruction of any of the rights and freedoms set forth.

The United Nations Covenants on Human Rights

After many years work the General Assembly in 1966 adopted two international covenants designed to transform the provisions of the Declaration of Human Rights into international law. Both covenants came into force in 1976 and are now legally binding on the nations who ratified them – about 45 in number, including Britain.

Responsibility for United Nations work concerning human rights is entrusted to the Economic and Social Council which reports to the General Assembly.

Resources

The central office of each organisation is given, but in some cases it would be a good idea to get in touch with your local branch. Sometimes this will be in the local telephone directory or can be found through the public library. When it is not, however, you can always write to the head office and ask for this information. You should always enclose a stamped self-addressed envelope. (The number on the left refers to the chapter.)

3   Gingerbread (An Association for One Parent Families), 35 Wellington Street, London WC2E 7BN. Tel: 01-240 0953
National Council for One Parent Families, 255 Kentish Town Road, London NW5 2LX. Tel: 01-267 1361

4   ALBSU, 'Adult Literacy: The First Decade', Kingsbourne House, 229/231 High Holborn, London WC1V 7DA. Tel: 01-405 4017
National Association of Citizens Advice Bureaux, 115 Pentonville Road, London N1. Tel: 01-833 2181 (Try Citizens Advice Bureaux in your area for information about classes for illiterate people.)

6   National Viewers' and Listeners' Association, Ardleigh, Colchester, Essex CO7 7RH (President: Mrs Mary Whitehouse; they publish pamphlets and a paper on pornography and obscenity in the arts.)

8   Catholic Marriage Advisory Council, 15 Lansdowne Road, Holland Park, London W11 3AJ. Tel: 01-727 0141
Jewish Marriage Council, 529b Finchley Road, London NW3.
National Marriage Guidance Council, Herbert Gray College, Little Church Street, Rugby, Warwickshire CV21 3AP. (For information about local addresses.)

9   Abortion Law Reform Association, 88 Islington High Street, London N1 8EG. Tel: 01-359 5200
Family Planning Information Service, 27–35 Mortimer Street, London W1N 7RJ. Tel: 01-636 7866
Society for the Protection of Unborn Children, 7 Tufton Street, Westminster, London SW1P 3QN. Tel: 01-222 5845

11   British Council of Churches: Community and Race Relations Unit, 2 Eaton Gate, London SW1W 9BL. Tel: 01-730 9611
Child Poverty Action Group, 1 Macklin Street, London WC2B 5NH. Tel: 01-242 3225
Commission for Racial Equality, Elliot House, 10–12 Allington Street, London SW1E 5EH. Tel: 01-828 7022
Corrymeela Link, P.O. Box 118, Reading RG1 1SL. Tel: 0734-589800
Equal Opportunities Commission, Overseas House, Quay Street, Manchester M3 3HN.
Institute of Race Relations, 247 Pentonville Road, London N1.
Minority Rights Group, 29 Craven Street, London WC2N 5NT. Tel: 01-930 6659

12   Job Change Project, 318 Summer Lane, Birmingham B19 3RL. Tel: 021-359 6596
Manpower Services Commission, Moorfoot, Sheffield S1 4PQ.

13   National Council for Voluntary Organisations, 26 Bedford Square, London WC1B 3HU. Tel: 01-636 4066. (Contact for free notes on opportunities for voluntary work. Also publish a Directory.)
National Youth Bureau, 17–23 Albion Street, Leicester LE1 6GD. Tel: 0533-554775. (They publish a guide to voluntary work opportunities.)

14   Gamblers Anonymous – see local telephone directory.

15   A-Care – Association of Christians involved in Addiction, Rehabilitation and Education, 4 Southampton Row, London WC1B 4AA
Alcoholics Anonymous, P.O. Box 514, 11 Redcliffe Gardens, London SW10 9BQ. Tel: 01-352 9779. (Look in your local telephone directory for one in your area.)

Churches Council on Alcohol and Drugs, 4 Southampton Row, London WC1B 4AA.
Health Education Council, Education and Training Division, 78 New Oxford Street, London WC1A 1AH.
Institute for the Study of Drug Dependence, 1–4 Hatton Place, Hatton Garden, London EC1N 8ND.
National Campaign Against Solvent Abuse, 345a Cold Harbour Lane, London SW9 8RR.

16 Beauty Without Cruelty, 1 Calverley Park, Tunbridge Wells, Kent TN1 2SG. (Promotes and supplies artificial furs and cosmetics that have no animal ingredients and have not been tested on animals.)
Compassion in World Farming, 20 Lavant Street, Petersfield, Hampshire GU32 3EW.
Dr Barnardo's, Tanners Lane, Barkingside, Ilford, Essex.
FRAME (Fund for the Replacement of Animals in Medical Experiments), 5B The Poultry, Bank Place, Nottingham NG1 2JR. (There is an official All Party Parliamentary Group for FRAME.)
National Anti-Vivisection Society, 51 Harley Street, London W1N 1DD.
National Children's Home, 85 Highbury Park, London N5 1UD.
NSPCC (National Society for the Prevention of Cruelty to Children), 1 Riding House Street, London W1P 8AA.
RSPCA (Royal Society for the Prevention of Cruelty to Animals), Education Department, Causeway, Horsham, Sussex RH12 1HG. Tel: 0403-64181

17 NACRO (National Association for the Care and Resettlement of Offenders), 169 Clapham Road, London SW9 0PU. Tel: 01-582 6500
NCCL (National Council for Civil Liberties), 21 Tabard Street, London SE1 4LA. Tel: 01-403 3888

18 Amnesty International, 1 Easton Street, London WC1X 8DJ. Tel: 01-833 1771
Co-operative Development Agency, Broadmead House, 21 Panton Street, London SW1.
Industrial Common Ownership Movement, 7–8 The Corn Exchange, Leeds LS1 7BP.
See local telephone directory for offices of political parties.

19 Age Concern, Bernard Sunley House, Pitcairn Road, Mitcham, Surrey CR4 3LL.
Community Service Volunteers, 237 Pentonville Road, London N1 9NJ. Tel: 01-278 6601
Help the Aged, Education Department, 318 St Pauls Road, London N1.
International Youth Year Co-ordinating Committee, 57 Chalton Street, London NW1 1HU.
Leonard Cheshire Homes, 26 Maunsel Street, London SW1.
National Cyrenians, 13 Wincheap, Canterbury, Kent CT1 3TB. (An organisation with many groups around the country, which cares for homeless people.)
RADAR (Royal Association for Disability and Rehabilitation), 25 Mortimer Street, London W1N 8AB. Tel: 01-637 5400
St John Ambulance, 1 Grosvenor Crescent, London SW1X 7EF.
Shelter, 157 Waterloo Road, London SE1 8XF. Tel: 01-633 9377
The Sue Ryder Foundation for the care of the sick and disabled, Cavendish, Suffolk.

20 CND (Campaign for Nuclear Disarmament), 11 Goodwin Street, London N4 3HQ. Tel: 01-263 0977
Centre for Peace Studies, St Martin's College, Lancaster LA1 3JD. (Information about Environmental Studies, Human Rights, Development Education.)
Christian CND, 22–24 Underwood Street, London N1 7JG. Tel: 01-250 4010
Conservative Research Department, 32 Smith Square, Westminster, London SW1P 3HH.
Nuclear Weapons Freeze, 82 Colston Street, Bristol BS1 5BB.

21 British Volunteer Programme, 22 Coleman Fields, London N1 (incorporating CIIR Overseas Programme, International Voluntary Service, UNA International Service and Voluntary Service Overseas).
CIIR (Catholic Institute for International Relations), 22 Coleman Fields, London N1.
Centre for World Development Education, Regent's College, Inner Circle, Regent's Park, London NW1 4NS. (Major source of teaching materials on world hunger and development.)
Christian Aid, P.O. Box no. 1, London SW9 8BH. Tel: 01-733 5500

Conservation Society, 12a Guildford Street, Chertsey, Surrey KT16 9BQ.
Friends of the Earth, 377 City Road, London EC1V 1NA. Tel: 01-837 0731
Intermediate Technology, 9 King Street, London WC2E 8HW. Tel: 01-836 9434
Oxfam, 274 Banbury Road, Oxford OX2 7DZ. Tel: 0865-56777
Save the Children Fund, Mary Datchelor House, 17 Grove Lane, London SE5. Tel: 01-703 5400
Third World First, National Student Movement against world poverty and under development, 232 Cowley Road, Oxford OX4 1UH.
United Nations Association, 3 Whitehall Court, London SW1A 2EL.
UNICEF (United Nations Children's Fund), 55–56 Lincolns Inn Fields, London WC2A 3NB. Tel: 01-405 5592
War on Want, 1 London Bridge Street, London SE1.
World Development Movement, Bedford Chambers, Covent Garden, London WC2E 8HA.
World Wildlife Fund, 11 Ockford Road, Godalming, Surrey.

24 British Council of Churches, 2 Eaton Gate, London SW1W 9BL.

25 The Samaritans, 17 Uxbridge Road, Slough SL1 1SN.

Further Reading

(The number on the left refers to the chapter.)

3 Hinton, Jeanne, *The Family in Transition*, New Christian Initiative Series, National Centre for Christian Communities and Networks, Westhill College, Selly Oak, Birmingham, 1984

11 —*Action for Justice and Peace*, Catholic Fund for Overseas Development and CIIR. (Helpful for starting and maintaining groups.)
Birnie, Ian H., *Four Working for Humanity*, Focus on Christianity – 3, Edward Arnold, 1969. (The four are Martin Luther King, Trevor Huddleston, Horst Symanowski and Dietrich Bonhoeffer.)
Evans, Robert A. and Evans, Alice Frazer, *Human Rights: A Dialogue Between First and Third Worlds*, Lutterworth Press, 1983. (Eight particular cases are taken. Each case is followed by commentaries on the situation described and teaching notes.)
King, Martin Luther, *Strength to Love*, Fontana, 1969
Noble, Iris, *Emmeline and Her Daughters: The Pankhurst Suffragettes*, Bailey & Swinfen, 1974
Pankhurst, Emmeline, *My Own Story*, Virago, 1979
Tutu, Bishop Desmond, *The Voice of One Crying in the Wilderness*, ed. John Webster, Mowbray, 1982

12 Nathan, Robert and Syrett, Michael, *How to Survive Unemployment: Creative Alternatives*, Penguin, 1983

15 Glatt, Max, *Alcoholism*, Teach Yourself, Care and Welfare Series, Hodder & Stoughton

16 —*Video Violence and Children*, Parliamentary Group Video Enquiry, 58 Hanover Gardens, London SE11 5TN. (First published in three parts.)
Midgley, Mary, *Animals and Why They Matter: A journey around the species barrier*, Penguin, 1983
Singer, Peter, *Animal Liberation*, Thorsons, 1983. (A classic on the subject of intensive farming and laboratory animals. Painful reading.)

17 Rose, June, *Elizabeth Fry*, Macmillan, 1980 (pbk 1981)

18 Easwaran, Eknath, *Gandhi the Man*, Turnstone Press, Wellingborough, Northants.

19 —*Voluntary Social Service: A Handbook of Information and Directory of Organisations*, a National Council of Social Service publication

Gundrey, Elizabeth, *Sparing Time: An Observer Guide for Helping Others*, Unwin Paperbacks, 1981

Muggeridge, Malcolm, *Something Beautiful for God: Mother Teresa of Calcutta*, Fontana, 1972

Owen, Roger J., *I Wish He Was Black: The Story of Trevor Huddleston*, Faith in Action Series, Religious Education Press, 1978

20 —*The Church and the Bomb* (The Report of a Working Party under the Chairmanship of the Bishop of Salisbury), Hodder & Stoughton, 1982

—*Common Security: A Programme for Disarmament* (The Report of the Independent Commission on Disarmament and Security Issues under the Chairmanship of Olaf Palme), Pan, 1982

Bentley, James, *Martin Niemoeller*, Oxford University Press, 1984

Blackwood, Caroline, *On the Perimeter*, Fontana, 1984. (Caroline Blackwood visited Greenham Common for the first time in March 1984. She talked to the women at the peace camp, bystanders, shopkeepers and members of RAGE – Ratepayers Against Greenham Encampments.)

Mountbatten, Lord and others, *Apocalypse Now?*, Spokesman Bks (for the Atlantic Peace Foundation in support of the World Disarmament Campaign), 1980

Wilson, Andrew, *The Disarmer's Handbook of Military Technology and Organisation*, Penguin, 1983. (Andrew Wilson is an Associate Editor of the Observer, where he was also defence correspondent for sixteen years.)

21 —*North–South: A Programme for Survival* (The Report of the Independent Commission on International Development Issues under the Chairmanship of Willy Brandt), Pan, 1980

—*Real Aid: A Strategy for Britain* (The Report of the Independent Group on British Aid under the Chairmanship of Professor Charles Elliott), Independent Group, 1982. (Distributed by Oxfam, Christian Aid, World Development Movement, Overseas Development Institute.)

Allen, Robert, *How to Save the World: Strategy for World Conservation*, Kogan Page, 1980

Joyce, James Avery, *One Increasing Purpose: The United Nations since 1945*, Christopher Davies, 1984

Kirk, Geoffrey (ed.), *Schumacher on Energy*, Abacus, 1983

Porritt, Jonathon, *Seeing Green: The Politics of Ecology Explained*, Basil Blackwell, 1984

Schell, Jonathan, *The Fate of the Earth*, Pan, 1982

Schumacher, E.F., *Small is Beautiful*, Abacus, 1974

22 Cassidy, Sheila, *Audacity to Believe*, Fount, 1978

Seed, Pat, *Another Day*, Heinemann, 1984

Seed, Pat, *One Day at a Time*, Heinemann, 1979

23 Nouwen, Henri J.M. and others, *Compassion: A Reflection on the Christian Life*, Darton, Longman & Todd, 1982. (Illustrated by a Paraguayan artist, Joel Filartiga, in memory of his son who was tortured to death by a police squad in 1976.)

25 Boulay, Shirley du, *Cicely Saunders: The Founder of the Modern Hospice Movement*, Hodder & Stoughton, 1984

Reports and magazines

The International Institute for Environment and Development (IIED) publishes a yearly report, also an Earthscan bulletin, 10 Percy Street, London W1.

The *New Internationalist* magazine, 42 Hythe Bridge Street, Oxford OX1 2EP. This comes out monthly and reports on the issues of world poverty and development.

UNICEF's 1985 Report, 'The State of the World's Children', Oxford University Press, lays stress on the fact that just four relatively simple and inexpensive methods could halve the rate of child deaths in the developing world and save the lives of 20,000 children every day.

Edward Arnold publish a series of information booklets called *Checkpoints* with titles such as *Peace and War*, *Human Rights*, *Prejudice* and *Drug Takers*.

Index of Biblical References

Genesis
1:1–31	7
1:26–31	7
1:27	23
2:21–5	22
2:24	23
16:1–6	34
30:3	34
37, 40, 41, 45	81
50:20	81

Exodus
15:3	69
20:8–10	45
20:12	10
20:13	82

Leviticus
19:18	18, 19
25:18–22, 23–38	78

Numbers
35:16	82

Deuteronomy
6:4–5	18, 86
22:22–4	27
24:1–4	27

Ruth
1	19

2 Samuel
11:2–12:25	65

1 Kings
21:1–19	60

Psalms
8:3–9	78
25:4–10	87
104:5, 24	78

Proverbs
6:6–11	44
13:24	10
18:24	17
22:6	10
31:10–31	25

Isaiah
2:3–4	69, 73
11:6–9	81
53:4–9	81

Jeremiah
31:31–4	84

Amos
5:10–14, 21–4	60
8:4–6	60

Malachi
2:10	10

Ecclesiasticus
6:14–17	19
6:17	17
6:18	16

Matthew
4:1–11	67
5:3–12	86, 87
5:7	19, 59
5:9	69, 73
5:14–16	67
5:21, 22	73, 83
5:23–4	19
5:32	27
5:38–9	73
5:38–42	19, 59
5:38–48	56
5:43–8	19
5:43–4	73
5:44, 45	83
6:1–4	49
6:6	85
6:9	10
6:19–21	49
6:24	48, 49
7:1	73
7:9–12	10
7:12	8, 73
18:15–20	18
20:1–16	44
25:14–29	46
25:31–46	68
26:52	69

Mark
1:21–2	65
1:35	85
2:13–17	82, 84
3:31–5	13
4:1–9	16
4:25	67
4:38	44
5:30–1	44
6:3	44
6:7–13	41
6:31–4	44
7:9–13	10
8:31	81, 90
9:14–29	85
9:35	67
9:36, 37	10
9:38–40	41
9:42–9	22
10:1–12	23
10:14, 15	10
10:17–31	49
10:29–31	13
10:34	90
10:42–8	67, 68
10:45	81
11:15–18	65
11:25	19, 59, 83
12:13–17	65
12:18–27	90
12:29–31	41
12:28–30	86
12:41–4	49
14:32–42	85

Luke
2:21–4	30
2:41–52	10
3:11	68
4:1–13	67
5:27–32	41
7:1–10	41
7:36–50	38
10:25–37	18, 19
10:38–42	38
11:1–4	85
11:5–13	85
12:13–21	48, 49
15:11–32	15
16:19–31	48, 49
18:1–14	87
19:1–10	49
22:49–51	65
23:34	83
23:34–43	86
23:43	90

John
4:1–30	38
4:24	6, 7
7:53–8:11	27
8:34	84
10:10	86
11	38
13:2–17	67, 68
14:1–3	90
15:13	17
18:11	65
19:26–7	10

Acts
2:43, 47	56
2:44–7	67
5:27–9	65
12:12	86
20:7	45
20:7–12	86, 87
20:33–5	46, 67
22:6–11	90

Romans
7:18–19	85
8:2	85
8:28	90
8:37–9	90
12:9–18	87
12:21	84
13:1	65
13:14	87
14:3, 4	53

1 Corinthians
6:18–20	53
7:10–11	27
7:12–16	27
12:12, 13	38, 87
13	22
15:3–8	90
15:33–4	53

2 Corinthians
11:24–9	84

Galatians
3:28	38
6:7	82

Ephesians
4:26	18
5:18	53
5:21–33	25

Philippians
1:19–26	90

Colossians
3:12, 14	87
3:18, 19	25
3:18–24	10

2 Thessalonians
3:10–11, 13	46

1 Timothy
5:23	53
6:10	48

Philemon 19

James
2:1–4	38
2:14–17	78

1 John
1:5	6, 7
3:17–18	68
4:7–21	6
4:16	7

Revelation
1:10	45